Contents

Quality in Mental Health - Your Views

Report on Stakeholder Consultation
on Quality in Mental Health Services

PROSPECTUS©
PUTTING STRATEGY TO WORK

Published by

Mental Health Commission
St. Martin's House
Waterloo Road
Dublin 4

Tel: 00 353 1 636 24 00
Fax: 00 353 1 636 24 40
E-mail: info@mhcirl.ie
Web: www.mhcirl.ie

ISBN: 0-9549292-1-7

© Mental Health Commission, January 2005

Coimisiún Meabhair-Shláinte

Foreword

Towards a Quality Framework: Report on Stakeholder Consultations

Introduction

This publication brings together two core aspects of the work of the Mental Health Commission. Section 33(1) of the Mental Health Act 2001 places a statutory obligation on the Mental Health Commission to 'promote, encourage and foster the establishment and maintenance of high standards and good practices in the delivery of mental health services and to take all reasonable steps to protect the interests of persons detained in approved centres under this Act'. The Commission welcomes this statutory function and our Strategic Plan for 2004/2005 gives explicit expression to this key responsibility. The Strategic Plan identifies the vision of the Mental Health Commission as 'working together for quality mental health services'. One of the strategic priorities of the Mental Health Commission specifically refers to 'promoting and implementing best standards of care within the mental health services'. This covers the broad spectrum of mental health services from childhood through adulthood to later years.

The Mental Health Commission has also clearly stated its commitment to consultation with all the stakeholders involved in mental health services. This publication reports on the extensive consultative process undertaken in 2004 on defining a quality framework in mental health systems. Quality is an integral element of mental health service provision. Achieving this is a continuous and evolving process. This report shows that there is a high degree of consensus among all the stakeholders on what are the core constituent elements of a quality mental health service.

I wish to say 'a big thank you' to all those who participated in this consultative process – to those who made written submissions, to those who participated in the workshops and to those who attended the focus groups, often at considerable personal inconvenience. The ideas and views provide a valuable insight into what constitutes a quality mental health service. We will be building on the wealth of ideas expressed in this report.

I also wish to record the Commission's appreciation to Ms. Patricia Gilheaney, Director Standards and Quality Assurance for her commitment in leading and developing the consultative process to inform the quality framework for mental health services and to Ms. Gale Gilbert who provided administrative assistance and support. Our thanks also to Prospectus, who conducted the consultative process on behalf of the Mental Health Commission.

We look forward to working for and achieving together positive change within the mental health services, building on current quality initiatives and improving the experiences of all those involved in the mental health services in Ireland.

Bríd Clarke
Chief Executive Officer

Mental Health Commission
January 2005

Réamhrá

I dTreo Chreat Oibre Ardchaighdeáin: Tuarascáil ar Chomhchomhairlí Geallshealbhóirí

Réamhrá

Tugann an foilseachán seo le chéile dhá phríomhghné d'obair an Choimisiúin Mheabhair-Shláinte. Faoi Alt 33 (1) den Acht Meabhair-Shláinte 2001 tá oibleagáid reachtúil ar an gCoimisiún Meabhair-Shláinte 'bunú agus cothabháil ardchaighdeáin agus dea-chleachtais a chur chun cinn, a spreagadh agus a chothú ó thaobh seachadadh seirbhísí meabhair-shláinte de agus gach céim réasúnach a ghlacadh chun leasa na ndaoine atá á gcoinneáil in ionaid cheadaithe a chosaint faoin Acht seo'(aistriúchán neamhoifigiúil). Fáiltíonn an Coimisiún roimh an bhfeidhm reachtúil sin agus tugann ár bPlean Straitéiseach do 2004/2005 míniú soiléir ar an bphríomhfhreagracht sin. Aithníonn an Plean Straitéiseach fís an Choimisiúin Mheabhair-Shláinte mar "obair i gcomhar ar mhaithe le seirbhísí meabhair-shláinte ar ardchaighdeán'. Tagraíonn ceann de phríomhthosaíochtaí straitéiseacha an Choimisiúin Mheabhair-Shláinte go sonrach do 'na caighdeáin is fearr cúraim laistigh de sheirbhísí meabhair-shláinte a chur chun cinn agus a fheidhmiú'. Clúdaíonn sé sin réimse leathan na seirbhísí meabhair-shláinte ó leanaí go daoine fásta agus daoine níos sine arís.

Tá tiomantas soiléir tugtha ag an gCoimisiún Meabhair-Shláinte dul i gcomhchomhairle le gach geallshealbhóir atá páirteach sna seirbhísí meabhair-shláinte. Tuairiscíonn an foilseachán seo ar an bpróiseas comhchomhairle leathan ar tugadh faoi i 2004 chun sainmhíniú a thabhairt ar chreat oibre ar ardchaighdeán i gcórais mheabhair-shláinte. Tá caighdeán ar ghné lárnach de sholáthar seirbhísí meabhair-shláinte. Beidh próiseas leanúnach agus athraitheach de dhíth chun é sin a bhaint amach. Léiríonn an tuarascáil seo an comhaontú láidir atá ann i measc geallshealbhóirí maidir le cad iad na príomhghnéithe a bhaineann le seirbhís meabhair-shláinte ar ardchaighdeán.

Ba mhian liom 'buíochas ó chroí' a ghlacadh leo sin ar fad a ghlac páirt sa phróiseas comhcomhairle seo – leo sin a rinne aighneachtaí scríofa, leosan a bhí rannpháirteach i gceardlanna agus iadsan a d'fhreastail ar ghrúpaí fócais go minic ag amanna míchaoithiúla. Thug bhur dtuairimí agus bhur smaointe léargas luachmhar dúinn ar cad is seirbhís meabhair-shláinte ar ardchaighdeán ann. Beimid ag tógáil ar an réimse smaointe a léiríodh sa tuarascáil seo. Ba mhian liom buíochas a ghlacadh freisin, thar ceann an Choimisiúin, le Patricia Gilheaney Uasal, Stiúrthóir Ardchaighdeáin agus Dearbhú Cáilíochta as a tiomantas agus í ag treorú agus ag forbairt an phróisis chomhchomhairle chun an creat oibre ardchaighdeáin do sheirbhísí mheabhair-shláinte a chur ar an eolas agus le Gale Gilbert Uasal a sholáthar cúnamh agus tacaíocht riaracháin. Ar mbuíochas freisin do Prospectus a stiúraigh an próiseas comhchomhairle thar ceann an Choimisiúin Mheabhair-Shláinte.

Táimid ag tnúth le hobair le chéile ar mhaithe le hathrú dearfach a bhaint amach laistigh de na seirbhísí meabhair-shláinte, le cur le tionscnaimh ardchaighdeáin reatha agus le cur le taithí gach duine a bhfuil baint acu le seirbhísí meabhair-shláinte in Éirinn.

Bríd Clarke
Príomhfheidhmeannach

An Coimisiún Meabhair-Shláinte
Eanáir 2005

Executive Summary
Achoimre Feidhmeach

Background to the report

The Mental Health Commission, established under the Mental Health Act 2001, is an independent statutory body. One of its statutory duties is to promote, encourage and foster high standards in the delivery of mental health care.

In order to discharge this responsibility, the Mental Health Commission plans to develop and implement a quality framework for mental health services in Ireland. This is a framework for continuously improving quality in mental health services, which will encourage and foster high standards of care. The framework will be used by the Commission to support continuous improvement in the quality of mental health services.

The Commission intends to undertake this work in partnership with the various stakeholders with an interest in the quality of mental health services – people using the services, families, parents and carers, advocacy and representative organisations, voluntary organisations involved in the area of mental health, statutory and private providers, the full range of professionals involved in mental health services, government agencies, and the general public.

As a first step in developing the quality framework, The Mental Health Commission engaged Prospectus to design and manage a consultation process aimed at gathering the views and perspectives of all stakeholders as to what constitutes quality in mental health services. The quality framework will build on and encompass these different perspectives.

This report describes the findings from the consultation process, conducted over the period May – August 2004.

When developed, the quality framework will build on service developments and improvements implemented in mental health over the last number of years, as well as on the various quality initiatives already in place in individual service providers organisations and, more generally, in the system.

The consultation process

The consultation process involved an initial planning and design phase, undertaken in partnership with the Mental Health Commission.

The actual consultation involved:

- A series of eight consultation workshops, attended by sixty-six people from groups representative of the key stakeholders

- A call for written submissions, which led to the receipt of two hundred and thirty nine (239) written submissions, from a wide range of stakeholders

- Two focus groups designed to elicit the views of people who have no specific contacts with mental health services

A number of recent consultative processes and strategies were also reviewed.

The consultation was designed to gather a wide range of perspectives on:

- What constitutes a quality service for people using mental health services?

- What constitutes a quality service for families, parents and carers?

- What is needed to deliver a quality mental health service?

Among those using mental health services, there are many groups likely to have differing needs and expectations as regards quality. The consultation aimed to ensure an inclusive approach by inviting groups who would be in a position to bring perspectives on quality for adult service users, children and young people, people with a disability and mental illness, groups who may have particular needs on account of cultural or ethnic minority status, or difficult personal circumstances, the families, parents and carers of people using mental health services, service providers, organisations with an interest in mental health services (such as government departments and agencies) and members of the general public.

The findings of the consultation process – What constitutes quality in mental health services?

The analysis of the feedback from the consultation identified thirteen key themes, which capture the wide-ranging views of stakeholders as to what constitutes quality in mental health services. In relation to each of these themes, the report describes in detail the views of each of the main groups of stakeholders. The key themes emerging were the following:

Theme 1   *The provision of a holistic, seamless service, and the full continuum of care, provided by a multidisciplinary team, are essential features of a quality mental health service*

There was a strong consensus among the different stakeholders that a comprehensive, seamless continuum of appropriate support, matched to the individual needs of each person, and which can be drawn upon at any stage of a person's journey to recovery, is an essential feature of a quality service. The key elements of such a continuum identified by stakeholders were:

- Local availability of the continuum of support in every area

- Choice and range of interventions

- Community-based services

- A seamless service with continuity of care and support

- Multidisciplinary teams to deliver the services

Theme 2   *Respectful, empathetic relationships are required between people using the services and those providing them*

All stakeholders concur that positive, supportive, empathetic and respectful relationships between people using mental health services and those providing them are essential in a quality service. The experience of this relationship is critical in its own right and is not secondary to the treatment or care offered within the relationship. Understanding and empathy, the capacity of professionals to listen well, the commitment of individual providers, non-stigmatising service delivery, and the time available for individual consultations were among the facets of a respectful service identified by stakeholders.

Theme 3 *An empowering approach to service delivery is beneficial to both people using the services and those providing them*

It is not enough that the relationships between service users and service providers are respectful, understanding and caring. A quality service will empower the people who use the mental health services. It will accord them equality of status within the relationship with the service provider, enable them to take as much responsibility for their own health and well-being as they can take, and provide them with the supports they need to maximise autonomy, choice, and self-determination while using mental health services.

The main facets of quality in an empowering approach to service delivery were:

- Knowledge and information to support involvement

- Partnership in planning, review and decision-making

- Choice, rights and informed consent

- Access to peer support

- Mechanisms for participation – complaints procedures, advocacy, and structures for influencing policy

Theme 4 *A quality environment, respecting the dignity of the individual and the family, will result in a more positive experience*

Stakeholders see the quality of the physical surroundings as having a strong impact on those using services and on their recovery process. Part of the requirement of a quality service is to provide settings and surroundings that respect the dignity of the individual, ensure basic comforts, meet needs, guarantee an acceptable level of privacy, and at least equate with the physical and accommodation standards in other health services.

The aspects of the environment that impact on people's experience of a quality service spanned:

- The standard of physical buildings

- The appropriateness of the physical facilities and their 'fit' with the needs of particular groups

- The range of activities offered, particularly in long stay settings

- The quality of food and nutrition provided

Theme 5 *Easy access to services is key to a quality service*

All stakeholders share the view that quality and access cannot be separated. Access should be equitable. The service should be there when people need it, and where they need it. Having information about where to go and how to find what you need is a basic access requirement, but, even before that, people must know where to get that information. The systems for managing access such as referral paths, geographical units of service, and eligibility systems should facilitate the person, as well as facilitating ease of administration.

The core elements of a high quality service, from the point of view of access, included all of the following, in the view of stakeholders:

- Information about services

- Equitable access

- Ease of access

- Flexible, user-centred availability

Theme 6 *Receiving a skilful service and high standards of care are extremely important to people using mental health services*

The focus on the quality of actual treatment or care, and the outcomes of that care, was less prominent in the feedback from the consultation than material dealing with the quantity and availability of services, or the relationships experienced in the course of service provision. Nonetheless, high standards of professional care and treatment are seen as important elements of a quality service.

The main elements of quality noted in relation to this theme were the need for people to experience quality care to international standards of best practice, the quality of diagnosis and prescribing, and the need for recovery focused interventions. All stakeholders emphasised the importance of these in a quality service.

What constitutes a quality service for families, parents and carers?

Theme 7 *Families, parents and carers need to be empowered as team members, receiving information and advice as appropriate*

Families, parents and carers want to be part of a solution-focused approach to treatment, and to play a constructive part in the team aiding the person who is experiencing mental health problems. There were clear differences of view between families and service users about the level of involvement that families can legitimately expect to have in relation to knowledge about the person's illness, information about treatment, planning and decision-making.

Theme 8 *Effective family support services need to be in place to reflect the important role families, parents and carers play in a person's healing*

Families need a range of support services for themselves at various stages in their family's member's illness and recovery process. The main areas of support needed by families in a quality service, in the view of the stakeholders, are:

- Information, advice and being part of the team

- The family being empowered as team members

- Provision of a continuum of support services for families

As with people who use mental health services, families, parents and carers need to experience understanding, empathy and respect

Families, parents and carers expect understanding and empathy, and a respectful service. They want to be listened to carefully, and have their views respected. They want to be treated as equals with professionals and be shown respect, and be kept up to date with what happens to their relative.

What is needed to deliver a quality mental health service?

Theme 10 *Staff skills, expertise and morale are key influencers in the delivery of a quality mental health service*

As with many service organisations, human resources play a pivotal part in everyday activity. The key message from the consultation was that, above everything else, the staff delivering the mental health service influenced the quality of the experience. Therefore, for providers to deliver a quality service, they must have the right staff in place with the appropriate skills. In addition to this, service providers must recognise the important role staff play, by providing training and professional development opportunities to people working in their organisations.

The key aspects of human resource management identified by stakeholders as needing to be attended to in a quality service were:

- Effective recruitment and retention of staff

- Appropriate staffing levels and expertise

- Provision of high quality training and continuous professional development

Theme 11 *Systematic evaluation and review of mental health services, underpinned by best practice, will enable providers to deliver quality services*

Any organisation committed to providing a quality service should ensure that evidence-based practice drives the development of its services. Almost all stakeholders believe that systematic evaluation and review of services is key to achieving this. A common view held was that people using the service should be involved in the review. A quality service would pay particular attention to the following:

- The need for evidence based codes of practice

- Systematic monitoring and evaluation of services, with provision for service user and family inputs into review processes

- An organisational commitment to quality

Theme 12 *The right management systems and structures should be put in place to facilitate the development of a quality mental health service*

Quality in mental health services will be driven far more effectively if the right structures and systems are in place. Quality must drive the development of effective management processes. At the same time, management structures with clearly defined roles and responsibilities, which reflect the quality agenda, will enable staff to understand on a day to day basis how their job plays a part in improving the quality of the services. Aspects of quality management systems identified by stakeholders included:

• Good leadership, with a commitment to quality 'from the top'

• Effective management of resources

• Strong person-centred mission and philosophy

• Effective information technology systems

• Effective and innovative service planning

• Data collection systems to support planning

• Accountability systems

Theme 13 *The external environment in which the mental health services operate has an important role to play in developing a quality mental health service*

Inevitably, factors in the larger system beyond the mental health services and outside the remit of service providing organisations impact on the quality of mental health services. The main areas of wider system change, or action needed to support the development of a quality mental health service, which were identified by stakeholders, include:

• Improved levels of investment in mental health services

• The need for wide-ranging programmes to address public attitudes to mental illness and reduce stigma

• The need for programmes for mental health promotion

• A rights-based legislative framework

• A new mental health strategy

• Pushing mental health higher up on the political agenda

Recommendations to the Mental Health Commission – Moving towards a quality framework

Based on the outcome of the consultation process and Prospectus' experience in developing and implementing quality frameworks, Prospectus makes the following recommendations to the Mental Health Commission in relation to the development of a quality framework for mental health services:

1. ***The themes emerging from the consultation process should form the foundations for the quality framework.*** Based on the feedback obtained during the consultation process, a quality mental health service is one which encompasses the following eight themes:

   - Facilitates respectful and empathetic relationships between people using the service, their families, parents and carers, and those providing it

   - Empowers people who use mental health services, and their families, parents and carers

   - Provides a holistic, seamless service and encompasses the full continuum of care

   - Is equitable and accessible

   - Is provided in a high quality environment, which respects the dignity of the individual, his/her carers and family

   - Has effective management and leadership

   - Is delivered by highly skilled multidisciplinary teams

   - Is based on best practice and incorporates systems for evaluation and review

   In developing a quality assessment or "accreditation" process for mental health services, explicit standards should be set for each of the above themes and measures developed for each standard.

2. ***The Mental Health Commission needs to determine the broader support role it will play in fostering quality in mental health services*** (beyond a quality assessment or "accreditation" process). The Commission should consider the range of processes or supports it should put in place to facilitate the development of quality mental health services, such as training or consultancy support for service providers undertaking an assessment/accreditation process, developing standard complaint procedures, or establishing a process for 'mental health proofing' strategies and policies.

3. ***The Mental Health Commission should clearly define the scope of the quality framework,*** in terms of the range of service providers that will be included in the quality framework and in the associated accreditation process.

4.	*When defining the themes, standards and measures in the quality framework, the Mental Health Commission should draw on the experience of other organisations* that have developed quality frameworks, internationally and in Ireland. The Mental Health Commission should also make full use of the ideas put forward in submissions (received as part of this consultation process) regarding ways of measuring quality in mental health services.

5.	*The Mental Health Commission should outline clearly the objectives it wants to achieve with the quality framework*

6.	*The quality framework must be flexible* enough to reflect the diverse needs of people using mental health services, their families and carers, as well as the different nature and scale of organisations involved in service delivery.

7.	*The quality framework should be applicable across the full range of services* required by people using mental health services, families, parents and carers.

8.	*The quality framework should promote consistency in the service* across the country and across service providers.

9.	When designing the quality framework, the *Mental Health Commission should seek to anticipate some of the implementation challenges up front.*

10.	The Mental Health Commission should *use the opportunity presented by the launch and promotion of the quality framework to help to foster a more positive public attitude to mental illness.*

11.	The Mental Health Commission should *use the quality framework as a platform for increasing the profile of mental health in terms of national policies and priorities.*

12.	The Mental Health Commission should *engage in ongoing consultation with stakeholders,* not only in relation to the quality framework but also more generally.

13.	*The quality assessment or 'accreditation' process should become an integral part of the organisations involved in delivering mental health services,* rather than a separate programme that is managed separately.

14.	*Implementation of the quality framework should focus on results,* more than on process, and *generate real improvements* in mental health services.

15.	*The quality framework should be used as a mechanism for driving changes in mental health policies, practice and structure* at local, regional and national level.

16.	*The Mental Health Commission must drive the development and implementation of the quality framework strongly at national level.*

Next steps

Having considered the findings from the consultation process, and the recommendations from Prospectus, the Mental Health Commission has decided to:

1. Engage with other national bodies with a remit in relation to quality and standards, such as the National Disability Authority, the Irish Health Services Accreditation Board and the Health Information and Quality Authority (once established) to learn from their experiences in implementing system-wide quality initiatives. Also, a review of quality frameworks for mental health services implemented in other countries will be undertaken to identify lessons for Ireland.

2. Establish a Working Group to design the quality framework. The Working Group will include service providers and organisations representing people using mental health services.

3. Establish an International Expert Group to quality assure the output from the Working Group.

4. Consult with stakeholders to obtain their views on the quality framework, and refine the framework, taking on board the feedback obtained from the different stakeholders.

The above steps will be completed within a reasonably short time-frame (e.g. 6-9 months).

Cúlra don tuarascáil

Is comhlacht reachtúil neamhspleách é an Coimisiún Meabhair-Shláinte, a bunaíodh faoin Acht Meabhair-Shláinte 2001. Ceann dá chuid dualgais reachtúla ná caighdeáin arda i seachadadh chúram meabhairshláinte a chur chun cinn, a spreagadh agus a chothú.

Chun an fhreagracht sin a urscaoileadh, tá sé i gceist ag an gCoimisiún Meabhair-Shláinte creat cáilíochta do sheirbhísí meabhairshláinte in Éirinn a fhorbairt agus a chur i bhfeidhm. Is creat é sin chun cáilíocht is seirbhísí meabhairshláinte a fheabhsú go leanúnach, a spreagfaidh agus a chothóidh caighdeáin níos airde cúraim. Bainfidh an Coimisiún úsáid as an gcreat chun tacú le feabhsúchán leanúnach i gcáilíocht na seirbhísí meabhairshláinte.

Tá sé i gceist ag an gCoimisiún tabhairt faoin obair seo i gcomhpháirtíocht leis na geallshealbhóirí éagsúla a bhfuil leas acu i gcáilíocht na seirbhísí meabhairshláinte – daoine a úsáideann na seirbhísí, teaghlaigh, tuismitheoirí agus cúramóirí, eagraíochtaí abhcóideachta agus ionadaíochta, eagraíochtaí deonacha a bhíonn rannpháirteach sa réimse meabhairshláinte, soláthróirí reachtúla agus príobháideacha, raon iomlán de ghairmigh a bhíonn rannpháirteach i seirbhísí meabhairshláinte, gníomhaireachtaí rialtais agus an pobal i gcoitinne.

Mar an chéad chéim i bhforbairt chreata cáilíochta, d'fhostaigh an Coimisiún Meabhair-Shláinte Prospectus chun dearadh agus bainistiú a dhéanamh ar phróiseas comhchomhairle a bhí dírithe ar thuairimí agus ar dhearcaí na ngeallshealbhóirí go léir a bhailiú maidir le cad is ann do cháilíocht i seirbhísí meabhairshláinte. Tógfaidh an creat cáilíochta ar na peirspictíochtaí difriúla sin agus cuimseoidh sé iad.

Tugann an tuarascáil seo tuairisc ar na fionnachtana ón bpróiseas comhchomhairle, a stiúradh i rith na tréimhse Bealtaine – Lúnasa 2004.

Nuair a bheidh sé forbartha, tógfaidh an creat cáilíochta ar na forbairtí agus feabhsúcháin seirbhíse a cuireadh i bhfeidhm sa mheabhairshláinte le roinnt blianta anuas, chomh maith le tógáil ar dhreasachtaí cáilíochta éagsúla a bhí i bhfeidhm cheana in eagraíochtaí soláthróirí seirbhíse aonair agus, níos ginearálta, sa chóras.

An próiseas comhchomhairle

Bhain céim tosaigh pleanála agus deartha leis an bpróiseas comhchomhairle, a rinneadh i gcomhpháirtíocht leis an gCoimisiún Meabhair-Shláinte.

Is éard a bhí i gceist leis an gcomhchomhairle iarbhír:

- Sraith d'ocht gceardlann comhchomhairle, ar ar fhreastal seasca sé duine ó ghrúpaí a bhí ionadaíoch do na geallshealbhóirí lárnacha

- Gairm ar aighneachtaí scríofa, as ar fuarthas dhá chéad agus tríocha naoi (239) aighneacht scríofa, ó réimse leathan geallshealbhóirí

- Dhá ghrúpa fócais a bhí deartha chun tuairimí dhaoine nach raibh aon theagmhálacha sonracha leis na seirbhísí meabhairshláinte acu a fháil amach

Rinneadh athbhreithniú ar roinnt próiseas agus straitéisí comhchomhairleacha freisin a rinneadh le déanaí.

Bhí an comhchomhairle deartha chun raon forleathan dearcaí a fháil ar:

- Cad is seirbhís cáilíochta ann do dhaoine a bhaineann úsáid as na seirbhísí meabhairshláinte?

- Cad is seirbhís cáilíochta ann do theaghlaigh, do thuismitheoirí agus do chúramóirí?

- Cad atá riachtanach chun seirbhís meabhairshláinte cáilíochta a thabhairt i gcrích?

I measc na ndaoine a bhaineann úsáid as na seirbhísí meabhairshláinte, tá go leor grúpaí ar dócha go mbeidh riachtanais agus ionchais dhifriúla acu maidir le cáilíocht. Bhí sé mar aidhm ag an gcomhchomhairle cur chuige uilechuimsitheach a chinntiú trí chuireadh a thabhairt do ghrúpaí a bheadh i riocht dearcaí a thabhairt ar cháilíocht d'úsáideoirí seirbhíse fásta, leanaí agus daoine óga, daoine faoi mhíchumas agus a bhfuil meabhairghalar orthu, grúpaí a bhféadfadh riachtanais speisialta a bheith acu mar gheall ar stádas cultúrtha nó mionlaigh eitneach, nó imthosca deacra pearsanta, teaghlaigh, tuismitheoirí agus cúramóirí dhaoine a bhaineann úsáid as na seirbhísí meabhairshláinte, soláthróirí seirbhíse, eagraíochtaí a bhfuil leas acu sna seirbhísí meabhairshláinte (ar nós ranna agus gníomhaireachtaí rialtais) agus daoine ón bpobal i gcoitinne.

Fionnachtana an phróisis comhchomhairle – Cad is cáilíocht i seirbhísí meabhairshláinte ann?

Shainaithin an anailís ar an aiseolas ón gcomhchomhairle trí phríomhthéama déag, a chlúdaíonn tuairimí leathanréimseacha na ngeallshealbhóirí maidir le cad is cáilíocht i seirbhísí meabhairghalair ann. Maidir le gach ceann de na téamaí seo, déanann an tuarascáil cur síos go mion ar thuairimí gach ceann de na príomhghrúpaí de gheallshealbhóirí. Ba iad na príomhthéamaí a tháinig chun cinn ná iad seo a leanas:

Téama 1   Is gnéithe riachtanacha de sheirbhís cáilíochta meabhairshláinte iad seirbhís iomlánaíoch, gan uaim a sholáthar, mar aon le contanam iomlán cúraim, arna sholáthar ag foireann ildisciplíneach.

Bhí comhaontú láidir i measc na ngeallshealbhóirí difriúla gur gné riachtanach de sheirbhís cáilíochta é contanam cuimsitheach, gan uaim de thacaíocht chuí, arna mheaitseáil le riachtanais aonair gach duine, agus ar féidir tarraingt air ag aon chéim d'aistear téarnaimh dhuine. Ba iad na príomh-mhíreanna de chontanam den sórt sin a shainaithin na geallshealbhóirí ná:

- Fáil a bheith go háitiúil ar an gcontanam tacaíochta i ngach réimse

- Rogha agus raon na n-idirghabhálacha

- Seirbhísí pobalbhunaithe

- Seirbhís gan uaim le leanúnacht cúraim agus tacaíochta

- Foirne ildisciplíneacha chun na seirbhísí a sheachadadh

Tá caidreamh measúil, le báúlacht riachanach idir na daoine a bhaineann úsáid as na seirbhísí agus na daoine a sholáthraíonn iad

Comhaontaíonn gach duine de na geallshealbhóirí go bhfuil caidreamh dearfach, tacúil, báúil agus measúil idir na daoine a bhaineann úsáid as na seirbhísí meabhairshláinte agus na daoine a sholáthraíonn iad riachtanach i seirbhís cáilíochta. Tá an caidreamh sin a chleachtadh fíorthábhachtach ina cheart féin agus níl sé tánaisteach do chóireáil nó don chúram a chuirtear ar fáil laistigh den chaidreamh. Tá tuiscint agus báúlacht, acmhainn na ngairmeach éisteacht go maith, tiomantas na soláthróirí aonair, seachadadh seirbhíse gan aithisiú, agus an t-am a bhíonn ar fáil do chomhchomhairlí aonair i measc na ngnéithe de sheirbhís mheasúil atá sainaitheanta ag na geallshealbhóirí.

Téama 3 *Téann cur chuige cumhachtaithe i leith seachadadh seirbhíse chun sochair do na daoine a bhaineann úsáid as na seirbhísí agus na daoine a sholáthraíonn iad araon*

Ní leor go mbeadh an caidreamh idir úsáideoirí seirbhíse agus soláthróirí seirbhíse measúil, tuisceanach agus comhbhách. Cumhachtóidh seirbhís cáilíochta na daoine a bhaineann úsáid as na seirbhísí meabhairshláinte. Tabharfaidh sé comhionannas stádais dóibh laistigh den chaidreamh leis an soláthróir seirbhíse, cuirfidh sé ar a gcumas an méid freagrachta agus is féidir leo a ghlacadh as a sláinte agus a bhfolláine féin, agus tabharfaidh sé na tacaíochtaí is gá dóibh chun neamhspleáchas, rogha agus féinchinneadh a uasmhéadú fad a bhítear ag úsáid na seirbhísí meabhairshláinte.

Ba iad príomhghnéithe na cáilíochta i gcur chuige cumhachtaithe i leith seachadadh seirbhísí ná:

- Eolas agus faisnéis chun tacú le rannpháirtíocht

- Comhpháirtíocht i bpleanáil, athbhreithniú agus cinnteoireacht

- Rogha, cearta agus toiliú feasach

- Rochain ar thacaíocht piaraí

- Sásraí do rannpháirtíocht – nósanna imeachta gearáin, abhcóideacht agus struchtúir chun tionchar a bheith ar pholasaí

Téama 4 *Beidh eispéaras níos dearfaí mar thoradh ar thimpeallacht cáilíochta a mbíonn meas aici ar dhínit an duine aonair agus an teaghlaigh*

Feiceann na geallshealbhóirí go bhfuil tionchar láidir ag cáilíocht na timpeallachta fisiciúla ar na daoine a bhaineann úsáid as seirbhísí agus go bhfuil tionchar aici ar a bpróiseas téarnaimh. Cuid de cheanglas na seirbhíse cáilíochta ná suíomh agus timpeallacht a sholáthar a léiríonn meas ar dhínit an duine aonair, a chinntíonn compord bunúsach, a fhreastlaíonn ar riachtanais, a ráthaíonn leibhéal inghlactha príobháideachais agus ar a laghad ar bith a bhíonn comhionann leis na caighdeáin fhisiciúla agus cóiríochta i seirbhísí eile sláinte.

Réimsigh na gnéithe den timpeallacht a bhfuil tionachar acu ar eispéaras dhaoine ar sheirbhís cáilíochta:

- Caighdeán na bhfoirgneamh fisiciúil

- Feiliúnacht na saoráidí fisiciúla agus an 'oireann' siad do riachtanais ghrúpaí ar leithligh

- An raon gníomhaíochtaí a tairgeadh, go háirithe i suíomh fanachta fada

- Cáilíocht an bhia agus an chothaithe a sholáthraítear

Téama 5   Tá rochtain éasca ar sheirbhísí lárnach do sheirbhís cáilíochta

Tá gach geallshealbhóir den tuairim nach féidir cáilíocht agus rochtain a dheighilt. Ba chóir go mbeadh rochtain cothromasach. Ba chóir go mbeadh an tseirbhís ansin nuair a bheidh gá ag daoine léi agus san áit a mbeadh gá acu léi. Is ceanglas rochtana bunúsach é faisnéis a bheith ag daoine faoin áit le dul agus faoin tslí lena fháil amach cad atá riachtanach, ach, fiú amháin roimhe sin, caithfidh go mbeadh a fhios ag daoine cá háit leis an bhfaisnéis sin a fháil. Ba chóir go ndéanfadh na córais chun rochtain a bhainistiú ar nós conairí tarchurtha, aonaid gheografacha seirbhíse agus córais incháilitheachta daoine a éascú, chomh maith le háisiúlacht riaracháin a éascú.

Bhí na nithe seo ar fad a leanas, ó thaobh rochtana de, i dtuairim na ngeallshealbhóirí, i measc na gcroímhíreanna de sheirbhí ardcháilíochta:

- Faisnéis faoi sheirbhísí

- Rochtain chothromasach

- Rochtain éasca

- Fáil sholúbtha, úsáideoir lárnaithe

Téama 6   Tá seirbhís sciliúil agus caighdeáin arda cúraim a fháil fíorthábhachtach do dhaoine a úsáideann na seirbhísí meabhairshláinte

Ní raibh an fócas ar cháilíocht na cóireála nó an chúraim iarbhír, agus torthaí an chúraim sin, chomh suntasach san aiseolas ón gcomhairle agus a bhí an t-ábhar a bhí ag déileáil le méid agus fáil na seirbhísí, nó an caidreamh le linn sholáthar na seirbhíse. Mar sin féin, feictear go bhfuil caighdeáin arda de chúram gairmiúil agus de chóireáil ghairmiúil ina míreanna tábhachtacha den tseirbhís cáilíochta.

Ba iad na príomh-mhíreanna cáilíochta a tugadh ar aird sa téama seo ná an gá do dhaoine cúram cáilíochta ag caighdeáin idirnáisiúnta an tsárchleachtais a aireachtáil, cáilíocht fáthmheasa agus cóir leighis a mholadh, agus an gá le hidirghabhálacha atá dírithe ar théarnamh. Chuir na geallshealbhóirí ar fad béim ar an tábhacht atá ag baint leo seo i seirbhís cáilíochta.

Cad is seirbhís cáilíochta ann do theaghlaigh, do thuismitheoirí agus do chúramóirí?

Téama 7 *Caithfidh teaghlaigh, tuismitheoirí agus cúramóirí a bheith cumhachtaithe mar chomhaltaí den fhoireann, ag fáil faisnéise agus comhairle de réir mar is cuí*

Tá teaghlaigh, tuismitheoirí agus cúramóirí ag iarraidh a bheith mar chuid de chur chuige atá dírithe ar réiteach i leith na cóireála, agus tá siad ag iarraidh páirt chuiditheach a bheith acu san fhoireann ag cabhrú leis an duine atá ag fulaingt ó fhadhbanna meabhairshláinte. Bhí difríochtaí soiléire sna tuairimí idir teaghlaigh agus úsáideoirí seirbhíse faoi leibhéal rannpháirtíochta a fhéadfaidh teaghlaigh a bheith ag súil leis go dlisteanach i ndáil le heolas faoi bhreoiteacht dhuine, faisnéis faoi chóireáil, pleanáil agus cinnteoireacht.

Téama 8 *Caithfidh seirbhísí éifeachtacha tacaíochta teaghlaigh a bheith ann mar léiriú ar ról tábhacht na dteaghlach, na dtuismitheoirí agus na gcúramóirí i leigheas dhuine*

Tá raon seirbhísí tacaíochta dóibh féin riachtanach do na teaghlaigh ag staideanna éagsúla i mbreoiteacht agus i bpróiseas téarnaimh dhuine den teaghlach. Is iad na príomhréimsí tacaíochta atá riachtanach do theaghlaigh i seirbhís cáilíochta, i dtuairim na ngeallshealbhóirí, ná:

- Faisnéis, comhairle agus a bheith mar chuid den fhoireann

- An teaghlach a chumhachtú mar chomhaltaí den fhoireann

- Contanam de sheirbhísí tacaíochta do theaghlaigh a sholáthar

Téama 9 *De réir mar atá le daoine a úsáideann a seirbhísí meabhairshláinte, caithfidh teaghlaigh, tuismitheoirí agus cúramóirí tuiscint, báúlacht agus meas a fháil*

Is féidir le teaghlaigh, tuismitheoirí agus cúramóirí a bheith ag súil le tuiscint agus báúlacht mar aon le seirbhís mheasúil. Tá siad ag iarraidh go n-éistfear leo agus go mbeadh meas ar a dtuairimí. Tá siad ag iarraidh go ndéileálfaí leo mar dhaoine comhionann le gairmigh agus go léireofaí meas orthu, go gcoinneofaí cothrom le dáta iad ar a bhfuil ag tarlú dá nduine gaoil.

Cad atá riachtanach chun seirbhís meabhairshláinte cáilíochta a thabhairt i gcrích?

Téama 10   Is príomhábhair tionchair iad scileanna foirne, saineolas agus meanmna i seachadadh seirbhíse cáilíochta meabhairshláinte

Faoi mar atá le go leor eagraíochtaí seirbhíse, tá páirt lárnach ag acmhainní daonna i ngníomhaíocht ó lá go lá. Is é an príomhtheachtaireacht a tháinig ón gcomhchomhairle ná, thar aon rud eile, go raibh tionchar ag an bhfoireann a bhí ag seachadadh seirbhíse meabhairshláinte ar cháilíocht an eispéiris. Dá bhrí sin, ionas go seachadfadh soláthróirí seirbhís cáilíochta, caithfidh siad an fhoireann cheart a bheith acu a bhfuil na scileanna cuí acu. Chomh maith leis sin, caithfidh soláthróirí seirbhíse an ról tábhachtach atá ag an bhfoireann a aithint, trí dheiseanna forbartha oiliúna agus gairmiúla a sholáthar do dhaoine atá ag obair ina n-eagraíochtaí.

Ba iad na príomhghnéithe de bhainistiú acmhainní daonna a shainaithin na geallshealbhóirí mar ghnéithe nach mór freastal orthu i seirbhís cáilíochta ná:

- Earcú éifeachtach agus coinneáil foirne

- Leibhéil foirne chuí agus saineolas

- Oiliúint ardcháilíochta agus forbairt leanúnach gairmiúil a sholáthar

Téama 11   Cuirfidh meastóireacht chórasach agus athbhreithniú ar sheirbhísí meabhairshláinte, arna thacú le sárchleachtas, ar chumas na soláthróirí seirbhísí cáilíochta a sheachadadh

Ba chóir d'aon eagraíocht atá tiomanta ar sheirbhís cáilíochta a sholáthar a chinntiú go mbíonn cleachtas fianaisebhunaithe mar threallús d'fhorbairt a seirbhísí. Creideann beagnach gach ceann de na geallshealbhóirí gur meastóireacht chórasach agus athbhreithniú ar sheirbhísí an príomhbhealach chun sin a bhaint amach. Tuairim choitianta a bhí ann gur chóir go mbeadh daoine a úsáideann an tseirbhís páirteach san athbhreithniú. Bheadh aird ar leith ag seirbhís cáilíochta ar na nithe seo a leanas:

- An gá atá le finaise bunaithe ar chóid chleachtais

- Faireachán agus meastóireacht chórasach ar sheirbhísí, le foráil don úsáideoir seirbhíse agus d'ionchuir teaghlaigh sa phróiseas athbhreithnithe

- Tiomantas eagraíochtúil i leith cáilíochta

Beidh cáilíocht i seirbhísí meabhairshláinte spreagtha i bhfad níos éifeachtaí má bhíonn na struchtúir agus na córais chearta ann. Caithfidh cáilíocht a bheith ina treallús d'fhorbairt phróisis éifeachtacha bainistíochta. Ag an am céanna, cuirfidh struchtúir bhainistíochta le róil agus freagrachtaí atá sainmhínithe go soiléir, a léiríonn clár oibre cáilíochta, ar chumas na foirne tuiscint a fháil ar bhunús lá go lá ar an tslí a bhfuil páirt le himirt ag a bpost i bhforbairt cháilíocht na seirbhísí. I measc na ngnéithe de na córais bhainistíochta cáilíochta a shainaithin na geallshealbhóirí bhí:

• Ceannaireacht mhaith, le tiomantas do cháilíocht 'ón uachtar anuas'

• Bainistiú éifeachtach ar acmhainní

• Misean agus fealsúnacht láidir atá duine lárnaithe

• Córais éifeachtacha teicneolaíochta faisnéise

• Pleanáil seirbhíse éifeachtach agus nuálach

• Córais bailithe sonraí chun tacú le pleanáil

• Córais chuntasachta

Níl aon dul as ach go mbíonn tionchar ag fachtóirí sa chóras mór a théann thar na seirbhísí meabhairshláinte agus atá lasmuigh de réimse freagrachta na n-eagraíochtaí a sholáthraíonn seirbhís ar cháilíocht na seirbhísí meabhairshláinte. I measc na bpríomhréimsí d'athrú córais níos forleithne, nó gníomh atá riachtanach chun tacú le forbairt seirbhíse cáilíochta meabhairshláinte, a shainaithin na geallshealbhóirí bhí:

• Leibhéil fheabhsaithe infheistíochta i seirbhísí meabhairshláinte

• An gá le cláir fadréimseacha chun aghaidh a thabhairt ar dhearcaí poiblí i leith meabhairghalar agus chun aithisiú a laghdú

• An gá atá le clár do chur chun cinn meabhairshláinte

• Creat reachtúil atá bunaithe ar chearta

• Straitéis nua meabhairshláinte

• Meabhairshláinte a chur níos airde ar an gclár oibre polaitiúil

Moltaí don Choimisiún Meabhair-Shláinte – Gluaiseacht i dtreo chreat cáilíochta

Bunaithe ar thoradh an phróisis comhchomhairle agus taithí Prospectus i bhforbairt agus i bhfeidhmiú chreata cáilíochta, déanann Prospectus na moltaí seo a leanas don Choimisiún Meabhair-Shláinte i ndáil le creat cáilíochta a fhorbairt do na seirbhísí meabhairshláinte:

1. *Ba chóir go mbeadh na téamaí a tagann as an bpróiseas comhchomhairle mar bhunsraith don chreat cáilíochta.* Bunaithe ar an aiseolas a fuarthas i rith an phróisis comhchomhairle, is éard is seirbhís meabhairshláinte ann ná seirbhís a chuimsíonn na hocht dtéama seo a leanas:

   - Éascaíonn caidreamh measúil agus báúil idir daoine a bhaineann úsáid as an tseirbhís, a dteaghlaigh, tuismitheoirí agus cúramóirí, agus na daoine a sholáthraíonn í

   - Tugann cumhacht do na daoine a bhaineann úsáid as na seirbhísí meabhairshláinte, mar aon lena dteaghlaigh, tuismitheoirí agus cúramóirí

   - Soláthraíonn seirbhís iomlánaíoch, gan uaim agus cuismíonn contanam iomlán cúraim

   - Tá an tseirbhís cothromasach agus tá rochtain uirthi

   - Soláthraítear an tseirbhís i dtimpeallacht ardcháilíochta, ag a bhfuil meas ar dhínit an duine aonair agus a chúramóirí agus a theaghlach nó a cúramóirí agus a teaghlach

   - Tá bainistíocht agus ceannaireacht éifeachtach ar an tseirbhís

   - Seachadann foirne ildisciplíneach ardsciliúil an tseirbhís

   - Tá an tseirbhís bunaithe ar shárchleachtas agus corpraíonn córais do mheastóireacht agus athbhreithniú

   Nuair a bhíonn próiseas measúnaithe nó "creidiúnaithe" cáilíochta á fhorbairt do na seirbhísí meabhairshláinte ba chóir caighdeáin dhearfa a leagan síos do gach ceann de na téamaí thuas agus ba chóir bearta a fhorbairt do gach caighdeán.

2. *Caithfidh an Coimisiún Meabhair-Shláinte an ról tacaíochta níos forleithne a bheidh aige i gcothú cáilíochta sna seirbhísí meabhairshláinte a chinneadh* (níos faide ná próiseas measúnaithe nó "creidiúnaithe" cáilíochta). Ba chóir don Choimisiún réimse próiseas nó tacaíochta a mheas ar chóir dó a chur i bhfeidhm chun forbairt na seirbhísí cáilíochta meabhairshláinte a éascú, ar nós tacaíocht oiliúna nó comhchomhairle do sholáthróirí seirbhíse a thugann faoi phróiseas measúnaithe/creidiúnaithe, nósanna imeachta caighdeánacha gearáin a fhorbairt, nó próiseas a bhunú do straitéisí agus polasaithe do 'phromhadh meabhairshláinte'.

3. *Ba chóir don Choimisiún Meabhair-Shláinte scóip an chreata cáilíochta a shainmhíniú go soiléir,* ó thaobh raon na soláthróirí seirbhíse a bheidh sa chreat cáilíochta agus sa phróiseas creidiúnaithe atá ag gabháil leis.

4. **Nuair a bhíonn téamaí, caighdeáin agus bearta á sainmhíniú sa chreat cáilíochta, ba chóir don Choimisiún Meabhair-Shláinte tarraingt ar thaithí eagraíochtaí eile** a bhfuil creata cáilíochta forbartha acu go hidirnáisiúnta agus in Éirinn. Ba chóir don Choimisiún freisin lán-úsáid a bhaint as na smaointe atá curtha ar aghaidh in aighneachtaí (a fuarthas mar chuid den phróiseas comhchomhairle seo) maidir le bealaí chun cáilíocht sna seirbhísí meabhairshláinte a thomhas.

5. **Ba chóir don Choimisiún Meabhair-Shláinte imlíne shoiléir a thabhairt ar na cuspoirí is mian leis a bhaint amach laistigh den chreat cáilíochta**

6. **Caithfidh an creat cáilíocha a bheith solúbtha** a dhóthain chun léiriú a thabhairt ar riachtanais éagsúla na ndaoine a bhaineann úsáid as na seirbhísí meabhairshláinte, a dteaghlaigh agus a gcúramóirí, mar aon le nádúr agus scála difriúil na n-eagraíochtaí a bhíonn páirteach i seachadadh na seirbhíse.

7. **Ba chóir go mbeadh an creat cáilíochta infheidhme ar fud raon iomlán na seirbhísí** a éilíonn daoine a bhaineann úsáid as seirbhísí meabhairshláinte, a dteaghlaigh, a dtuismitheoirí agus a gcúramóirí.

8. **Ba chóir go gcuirfeadh an creat cáilíochta comhleanúnacht sa tseirbhís chun cinn** ar fud na tíre agus i measc na soláthróirí seirbhíse.

9. Nuair a bhíonn creat cáilíochta á dhearadh, **ba chóir don Choimisiún féachaint le cuid de na dúshláin feidhmithe a thuar ón tús.**

10. Ba chóir don Choimisiún **an deis a thapú ó sheoladh agus chur chun cinn an chreata cáilíochta chun cabhrú le dearcadh poiblí níos dearfaí i leith meabhairghalair a chothú.**

11. Ba chóir go mbainfeadh an Coimisiún **úsáid as an gcreat cáilíochta mar ardán chun próifíl na meabhairshláinte a mhéadú ó thaobh polasaithe agus tosaíochtaí náisiúnta.**

12. Ba chóir don Choimisiún Meabhair-Shláinte **dul i mbun comhchomhairle leanúnach le geallshealbhóirí,** ní amháin i ndáil leis an gcreat cáilíochta ach freisin ar bhonn níos ginearálta.

13. **Ba chóir go mbeadh an próiseas measúnaithe nó 'creidiúnaithe' cáilíochta ina chuid lánpháirtiúil de na heagraíochtaí a bhíonn rannpháirteach i seachadadh seirbhísí meabhairshláinte,** seachas a bheith ina chlár ar leithligh a dhéantar a bhainistiú ar leithligh.

14. **Ba chóir go ndíreodh feidhmiú an chreata cáilíochta ar thorthaí,** níos mó ná ar an bpróiseas, agus **go nginfeadh sé feabhsúcháin iarbhíre** i seirbhísí meabhairshláinte.

15. **Ba chóir go mbainfí úsáid as an gcreat cailíochta mar shásra chun athruithe i bpolasaithe, i gcleachtas agus i struchtúr na meabhairshláinte a thiomáint** ag leibhéal áitiúil, réigiúnach agus náisiúnta.

16. **Caithfidh an Coimisiún Meabhair-Shláinte forbairt agus feidhmiú an chreata cáilíochta a thiomáint go láidir ag leibhéal náisiúnta.**

Na chéad chéimeanna eile

Ar na fionnachtana ón bpróiseas comhchomhairle, agus na moltaí ó Prospectus, a mheas, tá cinneadh glactha ag an gCoimisiún Meabhair-Shláinte na nithe seo a leanas a dhéanamh:

1. Dul i mbun cainte le comhlachtaí náisiúnta eile a bhfuil réimse freagrachta acu a bhaineann le cáilíocht agus caighdeáin, ar nós An tÚdarás Náisiúnta Míchumais, Bord Creidiúnaithe Sheirbhísí Sláinte na hÉireann agus An tÚdarás Faisnéise agus Cáilíochta Sláinte (a luaithe a bhunófar é) chun foghlaim faoina n-eispéireas i bhfeidhmiú tionscnaimh cáilíochta ar fud an chórais. Chomh maith leis sin, tabharfar faoi athbhreithniú ar chreata cáilíochta d'fheidhmiú seirbhísí meabhairshláinte i dtíortha eile chun ceachtanna d'Éirinn a shainaithint.

2. Grúpa Oibre a bhunú chun an creat cáilíochta a dhearadh. Áireofar ar an nGrúpa Oibre soláthróirí seirbhíse agus eagraíochtaí a dhéanann ionadaíochta ar dhaoine a bhaineann úsáid as seirbhísí meabhairshláinte.

3. Grúpa Saineolais Idirnáisiúnta a bhunú chun dearbhú cáilíochta a dhéanamh ar an aschur ón nGrúpa Oibre.

4. Dul i gcomairle le geallshealbhóirí chun a dtuairimí ar an gcreat cáilíochta a fháil, agus chun an creat a mhionathrú, ag cur an aiseolais a fhaightear ó na geallshealbhóirí difriúla san áireamh.

Tabharfar na céimeanna thuas chun críche laistigh de chreat ama réasúnta gearr (m.sh. 6-9 mí).

1 Introduction

Mental Health Commission

The Mental Health Commission, established under the Mental Health Act 2001, is a statutory, independent body with a dual mandate – to protect the rights of detained patients and to promote, encourage and foster high standards in the delivery of mental health care. The mandate of the Mental Health Commission is outlined in the Mental Health Act, 2001 Section 33 (1), which states:

> "The principal functions of the Commission shall be to promote, encourage and foster the establishment and maintenance of high standards and good practices in the delivery of mental health services and to take all reasonable steps to protect the interests of persons detained in approved centres under this Act".

The Commission has embedded its role in relation to quality and standards in its Strategic Plan 2004-2005:

- The Commission's Vision is "Working together for quality mental health services"

- In its Mission statement, the Commission states that it … "is committed to fostering and promoting high standards in the delivery of mental health services, to promoting and enhancing the well-being of all people with a mental illness…"

- Its second Strategic Priority is "To promote and implement best standards of care within the mental health services". The Commission has identified three supporting objectives under this Strategic Priority, which relate to the development of high standards of care and codes of practice, involving consultation with stakeholders, and the development and ongoing audit of quality initiatives in the mental health services.

In order to fulfil its mandate in relation to quality and standards, the Commission believes it is essential that it works in partnership with the different stakeholders involved in mental health services – people using mental health services, their parents, families and carers, representative organisations, voluntary providers of mental health services, statutory providers, the full range of professionals involved with mental health, government agencies and the general public.

The national context - in relation to quality

Quality in healthcare has received considerable and growing attention in recent years. Some of the more recent developments in relation to quality are outlined below.

The National Health Strategy
The National Health Strategy (2001), "Quality and Fairness", is guided by four principles – equity, people–centredness, accountability and quality.

Establishment of HIQA (Health Information and Quality Authority)
HIQA is a new organisation being established under the Health Reform Programme. Its role will include:

- Developing Health Technology Assessment

- Promoting and implementing Quality Assurance Programmes

- Designing and developing Health Information Systems nationally

Accreditation (Irish Health Service Accreditation Board)
This is an organisation wide system of self assessment/external appraisal. It involves peer review at various stages of progress. The accreditation process began in 2002 with the acute sector. The plan is to roll out the process to other aspects of the health service including primary care and residential services.

National Standards for Disability Services (National Disability Authority)
Over the last two years, the NDA and the Department of Health and Children have been developing these standards, in consultation with stakeholders. It is envisaged that all organisations that provide services to people with disabilities and are funded by the Department of Health and Children will be assessed against the standards by an independent body, on a three yearly cycle.

Clinical Governance
There has been increasing emphasis on the whole issue of clinical governance in recent years. Clinical governance can be defined as a framework through which organisations are accountable for continually improving the quality of their services and safeguarding high standards of care by creating an environment in which excellence in clinical care will flourish.

Clinical governance is a whole system process, which includes all disciplines involved in patient care. Key features include:

- Patient centred care

- Good information

- Reduced risks and hazards to patients - creating a safety culture throughout the health service

Currently, there is no system-wide quality framework for mental health services in Ireland.

Consultation in preparation for the development of a Quality Framework for Mental Health Services in Ireland

The Mental Health Commission plans to develop and implement a quality framework for mental health services in Ireland. This is a framework for continuously improving quality in mental health services, which will encourage and foster high standards of care.

Mental health services include services for children and adolescents, adults of all ages, persons with an intellectual disability and mental illness.

Before launching into the design of the quality framework, the Commission wanted to seek the views of the different stakeholders in mental health in relation to quality and mental health services.

In April 2004, the Mental Health Commission embarked on a consultation process. In particular the Commission wanted to establish stakeholder views on the key question of *"What is quality in mental health services?"*.

Prospectus was engaged by the Mental Health Commission to design and manage the consultation process, which was conducted over the period, May – August 2004. The methodology employed is detailed in Chapter 2.

The messages from this consultation will be a key input into the design of the quality framework for mental health services in Ireland. The stages involved in developing the quality framework, and where the consultation process fits, are illustrated in the diagram below.

Key stages in developing a quality framework for mental health services in Ireland

The process beyond the consultation

| Mental Health Commission Strategic Plan 2004 - 2005 | Consultation process for the quality framework | Development of a quality framework | Implementation and ongoing evaluation of quality framework |

Timeline:

Mar 2004   May 2004   Aug 2004

Ongoing involvement from stakeholders throughout the process

Perspectives on quality

Each of the different stakeholder groups involved in mental health services has their own perspective on what constitutes a quality mental health service.

For example, the views of people using mental health services, their families and carers in relation to quality are often based on their own individual experiences and reflect the extent to which they feel the mental health services meet their needs. Health professionals' views on quality will often focus on scientifically defined needs and the proper use of treatments and techniques, whereas managers in service provider organisations often consider quality in relation to the productive use of resources.

The consultation process, outlined in this report, sought to explore in detail the differing views of various stakeholders involved in mental health services, in relation to the question of "*What is quality in mental health services?*".

The quality framework for mental health services developed by the Mental Health Commission should encompass the different perspectives on quality held by the various stakeholders in mental health services.

Objective and structure of this report

The objective of this report is to describe the findings from a consultation process, conducted over the period May – August 2004, with a wide range of stakeholders involved in mental health services. During the consultation, stakeholder views were explored on a broad range of issues related to quality and mental health services.

Stakeholder views on quality in mental health services were explored in order to inform the development of a quality framework for mental health services by the Mental Health Commission.

In essence, the consultation sought to understand stakeholder views in relation to three areas, namely:

- What constitutes a quality mental health service for *people using mental health services?*

- What constitutes a quality mental health service for *families, parents and carers?*

- What is needed *to deliver a quality mental health service?*

Chapter 2 outlines the methodology used to design and conduct the consultation process and the different stakeholder groups involved.

Chapters 3, 4 and 5 outline the messages from the consultation process in detail. They identify the answers to the three questions above, as expressed to Prospectus during the consultation process, and grouped under the themes which emerged repeatedly during the consultation. In these chapters, the views of different stakeholder groups (people using mental health services, their families, parents and carers, service providers, organisations with an interest in mental health services and members of the public) are clearly identified.

Chapter 3 describes the views of each stakeholder group in relation to *"What constitutes a quality service for people using mental health services?"*. Chapter 4 describes the views of each stakeholder group in relation to *"What constitutes a quality service for families, parents and carers?"*. Chapter 5 describes the views of each stakeholder group in relation to *"What is needed to deliver a quality mental health service?"*.

Chapter 6 contains Prospectus' recommendations on how the Mental Health Commission should move forward with the quality framework for mental health services. The recommendations draw extensively on the feedback obtained from stakeholders during the consultation. They also reflect Prospectus' own experience in developing and implementing quality frameworks and initiatives in different types of organisations. Finally, Chapter 7 outlines the specific next steps decided on by the Mental Health Commission in terms of developing a quality framework for mental health services.

2 Methodology

The consultation was designed, conducted and the analysis completed over a three month period, between late May and the end of August 2004. A Steering Committee was established early on by the Mental Health Commission, to work with Prospectus during the consultation.

Three distinct phases were involved in the consultation, which are described below. The diagram provides an overview of the methodology used to design and conduct the consultation.

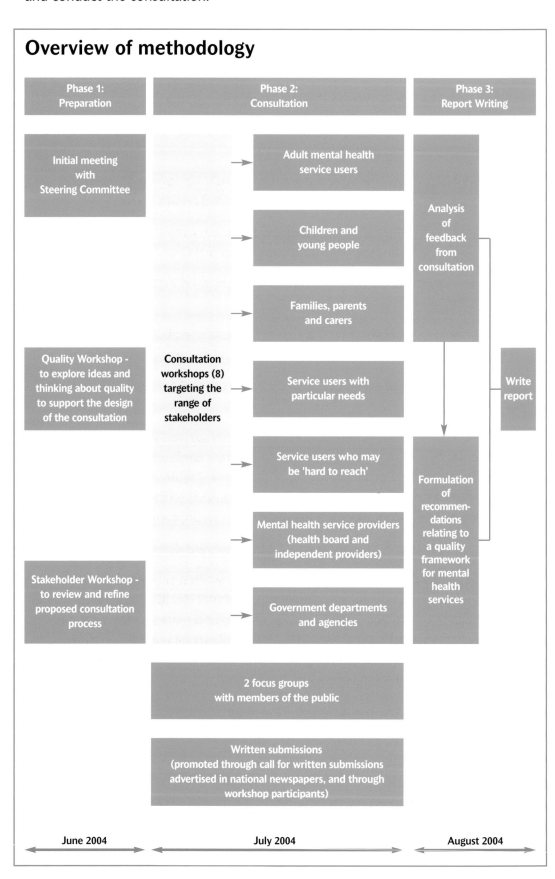

Phase 1: Preparation

During this phase, Prospectus designed and prepared for the consultation process. This involved:

- **An Initial meeting with the Mental Health Commission Steering Committee** to confirm the scope and objectives of the consultation process, the process for liaising with the Commission and the timetable for conducting the consultation.

- **A Quality Workshop** facilitated by Prospectus with the Mental Health Commission team to:

  - Explore the Commission's thinking in relation to quality

  - Present different quality frameworks used in a healthcare context, and the themes which underpin them

  - Understand how the output from this consultation process would fit into the longer-term plans for quality in the mental health sector

  - Identify the different stakeholder groups to be involved in the consultation and agree a definition of "mental health services"

  - Agree key messages/themes to be communicated in the consultation process

- **A Stakeholder Workshop** with a cross-section of stakeholders, facilitated by the Prospectus team and the Mental Health Commission, in order to:

  - 'Road-test' the proposed consultation process and get feedback on how it would work

  - Ensure that all the different stakeholders' perspectives – people using mental health services (children, adolescents, adults, older people, people with intellectual disability and special interest groups, such as people with disabilities or people who are homeless), service providers and families, parents and carers - were being involved in an appropriate manner

  - Begin to gather information about other relevant consultations

- **Drafting of the Questionnaire** to be used for written submissions. The questionnaire was developed jointly by the Mental Health Commission and Prospectus. An advertisement was drafted and placed in the national newspapers requesting submissions from people using mental health services, their families, parents or carers, service providers, organisations with an interest in mental health issues and the general public

- **Issuing invitations** to the range of stakeholders to attend the consultation workshops

Phase 2: Consultation

The consultation approach, outlined below, was customised to take account of:

- The wide range of stakeholders with an interest in mental health services

- The differing perspectives and requirements among stakeholders

- The tight timeframe available for consultation

In essence, the consultation process involved three key elements: the consultation workshops, focus groups and written submissions.

Consultation workshops

The consultation workshops were designed to provide stakeholders with an interest in mental health services with the opportunity to communicate directly their views on quality in relation to mental health services, in an interactive, structured and relaxed environment. These workshops provided us with rich and diverse perspectives on quality in mental health services.

Eight workshops were held during the month of July, each of which was facilitated by Prospectus.

Every effort was made to ensure that all the different stakeholders with an interest in mental health services were represented in the workshops. However, inevitably due to time, work and other pressures, it was not possible for some stakeholder groups to be present. Some of these groups, however, did contribute to the consultation, through written submissions.

The different stakeholder groups involved in the consultation workshops included representatives of:

- Adult mental health service users

- People using mental health services who may be 'hard to reach' on account of personal or social circumstances (including, for example, people who are homeless)

- People using mental health services with particular needs in relation to mental health (including for example, people who are deaf)

- Children and young people

- Families, parents and carers

- Voluntary groups, who provide support to people with mental health problems, advocate on their behalf and/or provide services to them

- Mental health service providers (health board and voluntary or independent providers of mental health services)

- Government departments and agencies (who provide services to members of the public, including people using mental health services)

A total of 66 people participated in the workshops. The names of the organisations represented at the workshops are included in Appendix 1.

At the workshops, participants explored:

- What constitutes a quality mental health service for people using mental health services?

- What constitutes a quality mental health service for families, parents and carers?

- What is needed to deliver a quality mental health service?

Workshop participants were also asked about any other consultations or initiatives, of which they were aware, which could be of relevance in relation to the issue of quality and mental health services.

Focus groups

Two focus groups were held (one in Kilbarrack in Dublin, and one in Blackpool in Cork) with the objective of providing a snapshot of the views of members of the public on quality in mental health services.

These focus groups were designed to elicit the views of people who have no specific contacts with mental health services. The same areas were explored as described above in relation to the consultation workshops. Individual members of the general public were also invited to make written submissions, through the advertisements in the national newspapers (see below).

Written submissions

A questionnaire for written submissions was developed jointly by the Mental Health Commission and Prospectus, and an advertisement placed in the national newspapers requesting submissions. The questionnaire could be requested by post or telephone from the Mental Health Commission and was available on the Commission's website. The questionnaire was also distributed to all organisations attending the consultation workshops. A copy of the questionnaire is attached in Appendix 4.

In total, 239 written submissions were received by the Commission as part of this consultation process. Of the 239 submissions:

- 5 came from members of the public

- 59 from people using (or who had used) a mental health service

- 71 from a family member, parents or carer

- 33 from a person involved in delivering mental health services

- 40 from organisations

- 31 were not attributable

Several submissions included the collated feedback from groups of people using mental health services, families and carers, or members of staff, with whom the organisation had consulted for the purpose of this process.

The list of organisations who made written submissions is included in Appendix 2. The names of the individuals who made submissions are not listed however, in order to protect confidentiality.

A number of submissions were made by individual staff members from named service provider organisations. However, because Prospectus did not wish to assume that these submissions represented the views of the organisations as a whole, they were treated as individual submissions, and the names of the individuals are not listed in the Appendix.

Phase 3: Analysis and Report Writing

During this phase, the findings from the consultation process were analysed by Prospectus, and recommendations for the Mental Health Commission concerning the development of a quality framework for mental health services were formulated. This phase involved:

Analysis of feedback from the consultation

Detailed analysis of the outputs from the different consultations, including:

- The eight consultation workshops

- Two focus groups with members of the public

- The 239 written submissions

The analysis was conducted by reviewing each output in detail and determining the key themes in relation to:

1. What constitutes a quality service for people using mental health services?

2. What constitutes a quality service for families, parents and carers?

3. What is needed to deliver a quality mental health service?

The views of each of the following stakeholder groups were collated:

- People using mental health services

- Families, parents and carers

- Service providers

- Organisations with an interest in mental health services

- Members of the public

Where appropriate, their views were captured under each of the themes identified. Chapter 3 describes the views of each stakeholder group in relation to *"What constitutes a quality service for people using mental health services?"*. Chapter 4 describes the views of each stakeholder group in relation to *"What constitutes a quality service for families, parents and carers?"*. Finally, Chapter 5 describes the views of each stakeholder group in relation to *"What is needed to deliver a quality mental health service?"*.

Review of other recent consultations

When conducting a consultation of this nature, it is important to build on other consultations or planning initiatives undertaken within the health services which have implications or findings which could be relevant to quality in mental health services.

A review was conducted of a range of recent strategies and plans on mental health services and on specific population groups (older people, Travellers, etc.), developed at national level and by health boards or other agencies. These documents were reviewed with a view to identifying any specific feedback from stakeholders in relation to quality in mental health services, which should be taken on board. The list of strategies and plans consulted is included in Appendix 3.

Formulating recommendations and writing the report

Based on the analysis above, and Prospectus' knowledge of quality frameworks in the health sector (and other sectors), Prospectus formulated draft recommendations on the key elements to be considered when developing a quality framework for mental health services in Ireland.

A final workshop was held with the Mental Health Commission Steering Committee to:

- Outline the key messages from the consultation process

- Discuss and review the draft recommendations on elements to be considered when developing a quality framework for mental health services in Ireland

Prospectus then completed the writing of this report.

Next Steps

The Mental Health Commission considered the findings from the consultation process and the recommendations from Prospectus, and decided on the immediate next steps (outlined in Chapter 7).

3 What constitutes a quality service for people using mental health services?

"It is important to realise that each patient is an individual and should be treated as so. Patient specific therapies are becoming increasingly important ... adequate provision for this should be allowed."
[member of the public]

"The benefits of a ... multi-disciplinary team ... include the ability for people to have their medical, social and psychological needs holistically assessed. It also means not having to repeat their "story" at different agencies ..."
[not attributable]

"I suffered from mental illness for approximately six to seven years and nobody advised me as to what literature to read to educate myself about my illness. I was for years being treated for a psychiatric illness which I knew absolutely nothing about."
[person who has used/is using a mental health service]

"The receptionist at the Centre was all important. The very first contact with the mental health services was a lasting experience. A genuine handshake and smile reduced the anxiety."
[not attributable]

"A nicer, brighter, more comfortable, less intimidating and less sterile environment that takes into account that these are real people who are frightened, lonely, vulnerable and ill ... would make the biggest difference to the quality of the service."
[family member/carer]

"Essentially mental health care should be an empowerment process. Only in this way can any care or treatment offered have any long term positive impact upon the lives of patients and families."
[organisation]

Quality in metal health service means ... *"Access and quality of care, irrespective of social status - wealthy or not so wealthy."*
[family member/carer]

"I am seen by a sympathetic, professional psychiatrist who has a genuine interest in my welfare. Appointments are regular, relatively punctual and easily accessible. When I needed the support of a social worker, I was visited regularly and a place on a course was made available to me during recovery."
[person using/has used mental health services]

"This a very busy clinic yet the staff always attend to the patient's needs, even at times without prior notice, in a very professional and efficient manner. The waiting room is consistently clean and tidy through the excellent staff efforts."
[not attributable]

"The doctor developed a good relationship with (family member) in that she felt he saw her as a person struggling with her diagnosis rather than just another sick patient. … He gave her the impression that he saw her and saw beyond her diagnosis, whereas successive doctors seem to have little interest in her health, lifestyle and recovery."
[family member/carer]

"I received a letter for an appointment with a psychiatrist in my local health centre last year. I had no idea what to expect. I had made the assumption that I would only see the doctor named in the letter and be out of there within 30 minutes. Instead I saw a nurse and a trainee nurse who asked a lot of questions and told me it was usual to bring a member of your family, I didn't know this and went to the appointment alone. I then saw a psychiatrist. After that I saw the psychiatrist named in the letter with the psychiatrist I had just seen and the trainee nurse. She spoke to me for about five or ten minutes from the other side of the room. She recommended an increase in medication; time spent in the health centre was about two and a half hours. By the time I did see the consultant psychiatrist I felt like I had been granted an audience with the Pope and I should be very grateful. However, overall the experience wasn't too bad."
[person using/has used mental health services]

Introduction

What constitutes a quality service for people using mental health services?

Themes and sub-themes emerging from the consultation

1 The provision of a holistic seamless service and the full continuum of care, provided by a multidisciplinary team

1.1 Continuum of care

1.2 Choice and range of interventions or treatment options at any given stage

1.3 Community-based services

1.4 A seamless service

1.5 A full multidisciplinary team to deliver the service and interventions at every stage

2 Respectful, empathetic relationships are required between people using the services and those providing them

2.1 Understanding and empathetic relationships

2.2 Respectful relationships

2.3 Reducing stigma

3 An empowering approach to services delivery is beneficial to both people using the services and those providing them

4 A quality environment, respecting the dignity of the individual and the family, will result in a more positive experience

5 Easy access to services is key to a quality service

5.1 Information

5.2 Equitable access and ease of access

5.3 Flexible service

6 Receiving a skilful service and high standards of care are extremely important to people using mental health services

Six themes emerged from the consultation process in relation to what constitutes a quality service for people using the service. These themes were emphasised by all of the different stakeholder groups during the consultation. The themes are:

- The provision of a holistic, seamless service, and the full continuum of care, provided by a multidisciplinary team, are essential features of a quality mental health service

- Respectful, empathetic relationships are required between people using the services and those providing them

- An empowering approach to service delivery is beneficial to both people using the services and those providing them

- A quality environment, respecting the dignity of the individual and the family, will result in a more positive experience

- Easy access to services is key to a quality service

- Receiving a skilful service and high standards of care is extremely important to people using mental health services

In this chapter, the views of each of the different stakeholder groups, expressed during the consultation, are outlined in relation to each theme. For some themes, a number of sub-themes were identified. In such cases, Prospectus has identified the views expressed by each of the different stakeholder groups in relation to each sub-theme.

The different stakeholder groups, whose views are outlined below, are:

- People using mental health services, including:

    - Children and young people

    - People using mental health services with particular needs in relation to mental health

- Families, parents and carers

- Service providers (i.e. providers of mental health services)

- Organisations with an interest in mental health services (such as government departments and agencies providing services to the public, including people who use mental health services)

- Members of the public

The consultation was designed to gather as broad and diverse a range of views on quality in mental health, as possible. In outlining the views of the different stakeholder groups, Prospectus sought to reflect this diversity and to capture all of the suggestions made (whether they were made by one or a large number of stakeholders). Where a specific stakeholder group is not mentioned under a given theme or sub-theme, this means that the stakeholder group did not explicitly refer to this theme or sub-theme during the consultation.

Theme 1

The provision of a holistic, seamless service, and the full continuum of care, provided by a multidisciplinary team, are essential features of a quality mental health service

The sub-themes, relating to this theme, identified during the consultation include:

1.1 *Continuum of care*

1.2 *Choice and range of interventions or treatment options at any given stage*

1.3 *Community-based services*

1.4 *A seamless service*

1.5 *A full multidisciplinary team to deliver the services and interventions at every stage*

All the contributors to the consultation process see the provision of a holistic, seamless service matched to the individual needs of each person, as a core element of a quality mental health service. This person-centred service depends on having a continuum of quality services in place in each area.

There were common understandings among people using mental health services, families, parents and carers and service providers about the nature of a holistic service. *People using the services spoke of a holistic service as meaning that the mental illness would not define the entire identity of the person who is ill. Families, parents and carers spoke about a holistic service as one where the person would be seen from the beginning as part of a family and a community. Service providers referred to the need to see mental health problems in a wider context and where the totality of the person's needs – medical, occupational, spiritual and physical – would be addressed as part of the holistic service.*

Individualised care planning was seen by all stakeholders as one of the key aspects of holistic service delivery. This will generate a proper fit between the care programme and the identified needs of the individual. Varying levels of support and treatment in line with needs (in particular high support needs) should prevent long-term involvement with mental health services.

There was strong consensus among the stakeholders that *a comprehensive continuum of support, where services can be drawn upon in line with individual need(s), at any stage of the course of a person's journey to recovery is an essential feature of a quality service.* While there were small differences in emphasis, this core view was widely shared.

The key dimensions of the holistic service raised by the contributors were:

- A local continuum of services that matches needs at various stages in the course of a person's illness and recovery process

- Choice and range of interventions or treatment options at any given stage

- Community-based services

- A seamless service, with continuity of care and support

- A full multidisciplinary team to deliver the services and interventions at every stage

Sub-theme 1.1 **Continuum of care**

Views of people using the services

For people using the services, the essential elements of a continuum of service span health, education and health management, counselling and therapy services, family support, personal development programmes, drop-in centres, day centres and day services, hospital services, occupational guidance, rehabilitation, education, training, housing and community residential facilities, access to peer support and the support of voluntary groups. Opportunities to avail of the support of family and friends were mentioned as part of the continuum.

For people using the services, access to housing and accommodation, in particular, must be acknowledged as one of the wider factors impacting on mental health.

When people have enduring mental health problems, the activities and facilities available to them in hospitals and other centres should offer variety and opportunities for development. Among the needs identified were activities such as yoga, drama, day trips, sport, access to a café and access to a library.

People want to have meaningful work opportunities in day centres and sheltered/community workshops, access to training programmes and courses, supported and sheltered work. These were all identified as part of the quality continuum of support.

Access to peer support groups and to the support services of voluntary groups are important elements of a quality continuum of care for service users. The benefits and positive experiences offered in these settings can make a big difference to people.

An emphasis on prevention should enable people to stay out of hospital for as long as possible.

Views of children and young people

Groups representing children and young adults want quality services geared to the particular needs of children and young people. There should be a strong focus on health promotion and prevention, and on community based services. Services like Childline and the Samaritans should not have to fill the gaps where mental health services should be available to support children and young people in distress.

The full spectrum of appropriate services and settings will be needed in order to provide a quality service. Appropriate settings for children and young adults are those that 'normalise' the use of the service, and the problems and experiences that bring young people to those services. Mainstream services like teen counselling and school-based services must be developed to a much higher degree – *the deficits in school-based counselling services were seen as a critical gap in the continuum of care.*

Views of people with particular needs

For deaf people, the critical element of the continuum of support and care is the capacity to be heard and to communicate effectively with service providers. In the absence of an effective communication mechanism, deaf people can become isolated, thus adding to the problems they face. In a quality service, deaf awareness and communication strategies will be addressed in professional training and development, particularly for GPs (General Practioners).

Deaf people who find themselves in hospital for long periods need support with communication, lest they lose their sign language ability and become isolated.

For people dealing with addictions and mental health problems, the first 'hurdle' to engaging with services is experienced in the access barriers that are seen as arising from the official definitions of mental illness, which appear to exclude people with personality disorders. The responsibility of the mental health services for people with dual diagnosis needs to be clarified.

For Travellers, it is essential that the service provision is culturally appropriate, and geared to the needs of nomadic families.

For people who are marginalised as a result of their chaotic lifestyles or on account of homelessness, continuity of care and outreach services are an especially important part of the continuum of care in a quality service – "*once contact is lost, the situation deteriorates rapidly*". Outreach teams for homeless shelters and linkages between GPs and hostel workers are needed.

The key people in the lives of homeless people or refugees and asylum seeking people who are alone, who can offer a substitute family group in the community, should be identified by providers.

Views of families, parents and carers

Families identified a similarly wide range of services as essential components of a quality continuum of support and care for people with mental health problems.

The spectrum of services identified ranged across early intervention services, community education, family support, counselling, crisis teams, day services, hospital services, training and employment support, housing and accommodation, long term support systems, and community-based facilities for early diagnosis, intervention, and continuing care.

Like people who use mental health services, families are concerned that the activities offered to people while in hospital for periods of time or attending day centres should be of a high quality. Quality activities are those that address self-esteem, accommodate personal preferences, develop skills, and address problems such as personal hygiene.

Training programmes should also develop skills and talents, and improve people's capacities for independent living. Activities in day centres should be age appropriate. Activities such as art, cookery and gardening could tap into people's talents and extend their experiences.

Families, parents and carers also stressed the importance of housing and accommodation as a key element of the continuum of support. A graduated range of accommodation options, including residential care, transitional accommodation, group homes and supported living accommodation, should be part of the continuum. No person should leave hospital without an accommodation plan. The quality of supervision in sheltered accommodation settings would be part of a quality service.

Facilitated support groups should be available, where people can give each other support in a family setting.

Families, parents and carers want to see closer integration of physical care with mental health care. Dental care, eye care, nutrition and weight control should be monitored as part of the holistic approach to service provision.

Views of service providers

Service providers' view of the essential continuum of care was very similar to that identified by people using mental health services and by their families and carers. They described the complex range of services needed, from mental health promotion for the population at large, through to follow up and support for individuals. ***A proactive focus on mental health for the population, as distinct from merely responding to mental ill-health, should be a core element of a quality service.***

According to service providers, both school and workplace counselling should form part of a support service, as part of prevention and early intervention.

Service providers see access to both mainstream and specialist services as important. People should be able to access both at the same time, if that is what the person needs. A structure is needed to enable people to be put in touch with mainstream services such as FÁS.

Like the other stakeholders, service providers identified the need for quality experiences for people in sheltered work or day activity settings, and for a diversity of programmes, which should include therapeutic as well as occupational elements. These activities should facilitate self-esteem, skill development and confidence building. They should facilitate people in making the journey to recovery and help people to resume their place in society. Activities such as yoga, massage, tai chi should be available, as these options become accepted as part of mainstream community activity. People of similar ages should be located together in the services.

Community education and community interaction programmes should form part of the programme of services in every area. Respite services, home care services, outreach teams targeting 'high risk' individuals, and therapy groups should also form part of the continuum. Day services for people over sixty-five were identified as a particular gap.

A definite care plan, agreed with the person with mental health problems, and significant others in their lives, should explain in detail the services to be accessed as part of the next stages of support.

The role of support groups and client-led groups needs to be acknowledged as an integral part of a quality service. The support groups have a role in offering assistance to individuals and in campaigning. Providers need to build links with these groups. Like families, service providers see a closer integration of physical healthcare with mental healthcare as an element of quality service.

Views of organisations with an interest in mental health

These organisations also stressed the need for a continuum of care. Elements mentioned in particular were:

- Graded levels of support to fit the person's need at any given time

- Follow up and review of individual care plans

- Education, particularly for children in hospital

- Services suited to the needs of children and young people

- Preventative mental health services for children

- Supervised hostels and apartments

- Respite care for families of children with chronic mental ill health

Views of members of the public

Members of the public identified the need for prevention, community education, step-down services and aftercare. Services should be part of a network of support. Call-in centres should be available where young people, in particular, can go if they feel they need help, as well as school-based services.

Sub-theme 1.2 **Choice and range of interventions or treatment options at any given stage**

Views of people using the services

People using mental health services want access to a wide range of options as part of their recovery programme. The main needs mentioned regarding a quality service in this regard were:

- Equal status should be allocated to psychological, rehabilitative and social care programmes as to medical care

- Access to counselling

- Access to alternative therapies

- Recognising that informal help is often what is needed rather than a doctor

- Involvement with support groups as part of the recovery plan

- Reduced reliance on medication – avoid 'pill for every ill' approach

- Holistic service which takes account of diet, social skills, education, training

There was a concern that a 'psychiatric model' of service may be particularly disempowering for children and young people. The risk might be that, in the development of services, this model could over-ride more suitable approaches, such as behaviourally focused models that locate and understand young people's difficulties in the wider context of their lives and the lives of the family.

Views of families, parents and carers

Like people using the services, *families mentioned the need for a variety of therapies and interventions offering a holistic and integrated service,* including counselling, group therapy, access to complementary therapies, stress management programmes, and greater reliance on possibilities of social contacts and group membership.

According to families and carers, a quality service would provide people using the service with a choice of consultant psychiatrist and a choice of treatment provider.

The need for a reduced reliance on medication was raised. The view was that **prescribing medication should not be the first option.** More time should be spent talking to people. For children and young people, a concern was expressed about young people taking medication too soon, and the need to "*try to talk before medication*".

Views of service providers

Access to non-medical forms of intervention and lower levels of dependence on medication as the preferred form of treatment, was raised by service providers. Access to counselling, occupational therapy and support services, parents' groups and children's groups in children's services, should form part of the repertoire.

Other related elements of a quality service were seen as:

- The provision of choice for service users

- Recognition of models of care based on different understandings of mental health/mental illness

- Variety in service delivery models and diversity in treatment options

- Access to counselling at point of recovery to address difficulties with relationships, low self-esteem and loss adjustment

- Use of treatments of proven effectiveness

Views of organisations with an interest in mental health

These organisations proposed that, in a quality service, there would be:

- Recognition of the benefits of social and psychotherapeutic options

- Responses that are not necessarily informed by the medical model

- A psychological model of care that may be more appropriate for children - not all mental health care for children should be provided through the medical model

Views of members of the public

Members of the public also highlighted access to non-pharmaceutical options as a mark of a quality service. **Access to counselling as a first option, before drugs are tried, was seen as important, especially for young people.**

Views of people using services

Community-based services should be available and organised around a "one-stop shop", with outpatient clinics, counselling and group therapy opportunities in a single location. As part of community-based services, people should have the option of home-based services.

Clinics should serve as information centres and provide an 'open house' for people.

Institutions should not be used for mental health care in a quality service, except as a last resort.

Community based services need to be accessible to people with mental health difficulties. There is often a lack of understanding and awareness among primary care professionals about mental health issues, in the view of people using mental health services.

Views of service providers

Service providers see a need for the full continuum of support to be available in each geographic area, as part of a quality service. They view a quality service as one that provides:

- Services in the least restrictive environment

- Community oriented services, supported by high quality acute services

- Acute care as the last resort

- Services where decision-making happens at the closest point to service delivery

Service providers referred to the need to avoid community provision in specialised locations, which stigmatise service users – a view that may be at odds with the concept of a one-stop shop suggested by some other stakeholders.

Views of organisations with an interest in mental health

Mental health services should start with primary care. In relation to children, children should only be admitted to hospital if the care they require cannot be equally well provided at home on a day basis. Minimising the length of stay for children in hospital presumes the availability of locally based community facilities to provide the necessary support, as well as the skills to facilitate home-based treatment.

Views of members of the public

Members of the public felt that *a quality service would be one where services would be provided in a manner that minimises the stigma attached to availing of mental health services.* GPs should have other members of the (mental health) team available in a health centre or in their surgery.

Sub-theme 1.4 **A seamless service**

The views on a quality seamless service covered **continuity of personnel, continuity of care and arrangements for review and follow-up.** The views also dealt with the arrangements for wider linkages between agencies, so as to facilitate a seamless service for individuals.

People using the services, families and service providers all identified consistent follow-up and aftercare as a particularly critical element of the continuity of care. In a quality service *"aftercare is the key"*. The provision of quality aftercare depends on the availability of services such as counselling, day care, support from the community nursing service, help with finding employment, outreach programmes and clubs.

Views of people using the services

People using mental health services see a quality service as one where they have continuity of care and support, from first contact to discharge planning and aftercare. They highlight the importance of consistency in the relationship with the person providing the service, and continuity of contact – *'a familiar face'*. Changing doctors frequently is difficult.

A mentor or support person is needed to help the person prepare for social inclusion. Good communication with the GP is also seen as part of quality follow-up.

Follow-up and support geared to the needs of Traveller families will be needed in order to address the problems of early self-discharge, poor compliance with treatment regimes (often due to literacy difficulties), and poor attendance at follow-up clinics, which have been identified in the National Traveller Health Strategy (2002-2005).

Views of families, parents and carers

Consistency in the personnel delivering the service facilitates trust building and confidence in the staff. There were repeated references to the problems that are caused for the person using the service on account of frequent changes in staffing, and in particular, the impact on the service for their family members arising from the six-monthly rotation of doctors – *'just when the doctor is beginning to get to know you'*. The service user needs opportunities to get to know the whole team, as well as the doctor.

Continuity of care, as well as consistency of personnel, is also important, in the view of families. Regular review, close monitoring and evaluation of the person's progress, and monitoring of the effectiveness of treatment are key elements of the service. A case management structure would help to ensure continuity of care.

Families, parents and carers want follow-up and aftercare planned as an integral part of discharge planning. The speed and continuity of support are the key ingredients of quality follow-up. The level of follow-up support should be high in the first year following a discharge from hospital, especially when the person has no family support.

Advice regarding recovery, access to counselling, and support to 'get back on your feet' and back to work are essential. A family should be able to access a call-out service if necessary.

Follow-up reminders about appointments, checks on appointments missed, and contact with carers to check that the person is taking their medication, would form part of a quality follow-up service.

Families identified the linkages and communication with services outside the mental health services as an element of a quality service. Linkages with the Gardaí, the Courts, the Probation Service were considered important, as well as contacts with voluntary agencies who may be able to offer support.

Views of service providers

Service providers stated that it should be easy for people to make contact with the service at any time. Service providers highlighted the importance of both the designated key worker and the care plan as a means of ensuring a seamless service.

Consistency of personnel offers the opportunity to build healing relationships. Ways are needed to avoid asking service users to repeat their story for different professionals. In this context, the problems arising from the rotation system for junior doctors were raised. Regular reviews of the person's progress by the consultant psychiatrist, and review meetings for parents (in the case of children) with the full multidisciplinary team were mentioned as features of a quality service. A key worker system would facilitate service co-ordination, as well as comprehensive case management systems in the community.

Service providers identified the importance of aftercare visits from an occupational therapist or care worker, frequent contact with appropriate staff, follow-up on failed appointments, and regular updates for the GP on the person's progress. Home visits and outpatient appointments, and the continued support and availability of clinicians were identified as important. A support worker should be available to help implement a relapse prevention strategy.

Systems for sharing data with other providers, good liaison between clinicians and other services, and formal forums with other service providers, for example in the emergency services, or in the education sector, are mechanisms for building essential linkages to facilitate seamless working at a wider level.

Views of organisations with an interest in mental health

These organisations also highlighted the need for timely responses and follow through, strong communication between providers and service users, and between acute and primary care.

Sub-theme 1.5 **A full multidisciplinary team to deliver the services and interventions at every stage**

Views of people using the services

People using mental health services highlighted the need to recognise the input of all professionals and specialisms involved in mental health services, and to have the full multidisciplinary team in place in order to deliver a quality service. In particular, reference was made to the *need for social workers, psychiatrists, general practitioners, community nurses, and occupational therapists as essential members of the team.*

A wider concept of team was also raised in the suggestion that qualified community workers should link with staff in centres. Support groups should be seen as part of teams.

Teamwork is important, as well as the availability of the team. The quality of communication among team members, and the importance of good teamwork were raised. The need for good linkages and communication between people using the services and local community mental health teams was raised.

The balance of influence among team members was raised, in that the consultant is perceived to have too much control. Linked to this is the need for equal status to be given to team members with psychological, rehabilitative and social skills expertise.

Multi-disciplinary teams skilled in working with children and young people are part of the essential infrastructure of a quality service. The concept of specialist services for young people should extend to young adults over 18, for whom adult mental health services are seen to be just as inappropriate as they are for children and adolescents.

Views of families, parents and carers

Families also specified the need to provide full teams to deliver a quality service. Essential team members include the psychologist, family therapist and family counsellor, occupational therapist, social worker, doctor, home care nurse, community psychiatric nurse, and support worker. The care team model should include carers.

In addition to 'general' teams, families identified some specialist teams as essential to a quality service. Home care teams and crisis teams should be in place. A team offering a 'wrap around' service for people with acquired brain injury, led by a neuro psychiatrist, should be in place. Multidisciplinary teams for people with Attention-Deficit/Hyperactivity Disorder (ADHD) are also needed.

Like people who use mental health services, families were interested in how teams actually work, as well as in having the team in place. Continuity within the team was raised, and speedy access to the team following diagnosis.

Full co-operation among team members and a team-working approach is needed for a quality service. *Families highlighted the need for communication between disciplines, for example, psychiatrists interacting with counsellors and alternative practitioners.* The links between GPs and the psychiatric services also need to be strong in a quality service.

Views of service providers

Service providers identified the presence of multidisciplinary teams and teamwork as key requirements for providing a quality service. People should have access to the full range of disciplines, and full teams with adequate staff.

Specialist teams are needed to provide a quality service to particular groups, including children. Aftercare teams should be in place, as well as home-based teams, early intervention teams and rehabilitation/recovery teams. Dedicated teams are needed for people with learning disability and mental health problems, particularly those with mild learning disability.

Membership of the team was raised and the need for comprehensive membership of all key players. Particular reference was made to medical staff, nursing staff, speech and language therapists, directors of nursing, area co-ordinators, play therapists (in the case of children), occupational therapists, and social workers. The need for community psychiatric nurses and GPs to be an integral part of the team was stressed, as was the overall role of the GP in co-ordinating the care of the person, within the wider context of family, work and community, as well as in relation to physical health.

Families and people using the mental health services should be seen as part of the team. A broader concept of team proposed that all staff engaged in giving the service to a client should be seen as part of the team, including, for example, child care staff, home help and drivers.

The commentary from providers tended to focus strongly on team dynamics as a dimension of providing a quality service. Views expressed included the following:

- The need for the team to operate as a fully integrated multidisciplinary team

- The need for interdisciplinary ways of working (interdisciplinary team working was explained as the members of the team working together and sharing expertise, in order to deliver a holistic service)

- The need for the team to work in a flexible way, in order to ensure support is available when needed

- The need for clarity about boundaries and clear role definitions

- The importance of teams operating in a way that offers collective support to team members

- Structures and policies to enable the team to work together

- Delegation of responsibility

- All staff involved in decision-making about services for a client

- Rotating chair of team

- Team co-ordinator in place

- Secretarial support for teams

The quality of the relationship among team members was raised as an important element of well functioning teams. *An effective team requires equality of status for all members of the team, respect for all members of the team, with the contribution and expertise of each member understood and valued.* Junior staff roles need to be acknowledged. The concept of each team member being viewed as a consultant to the other team members was proposed.

Acceptance of varying views and understandings within teams was seen as important to a quality functioning of teams. The readiness to share information was also raised as a determinant of quality teamwork.

Providers saw good communication across teams and different services as essential to the provision of a quality service, in particular:

- Networking among professionals

- Good liaison with support services

- Good understanding among different professionals about the skills of others

- Importance of communication between teams in different settings

- Need for development of both internal and external linkages and communication

- Communication between GPs and mental health professionals; communication aimed at ensuring that everyone knows about changes in treatment and diagnosis

- Greater sharing of knowledge and patient care

- Information on and clarification of the various roles and functions of professionals at every level of the service, for the benefit of both service providers and service users

Views of organisations with an interest in mental health

Teamwork was also mentioned by these organisations as a facet of a quality service. The need for all staff that come in contact with people using mental health services to have a good understanding of mental health issues was raised. Teams should be constructed to fit the needs of particular groups. For example, the hospital-based group should include a play therapist for children.

A community mental health team is needed for children and young people, including community psychiatrists, psychologists and GPs.

Views of members of the public

Members of the public felt that everyone needs a patient-specific service. Systems for review are needed to make sure that treatments are changed if they are not working. Teamwork is important and counsellors should be available as part of teams.

Theme 2

Respectful, empathetic relationships are required between people using the services and those providing them

The sub-themes, relating to this theme, identified during the consultation include:

2.1   *Understanding and empathetic relationships*

2.2   *Respectful relationships*

2.3   *Reducing stigma*

People using mental health services want service providers to recognise that the way they are treated as people, and the attitudes of professionals towards them, makes a big difference to them. All stakeholders share this view. ***The tone and warmth of interpersonal relationships between the person using the service and the person or team providing the service is a crucial element of quality.*** Stakeholders see positive, supportive, empathetic and respectful relationships as essential for a quality service.

Processes and work practices impinge on the possibilities for helpful and healing relationships. The quality of listening, the commitment of individual providers, and the time available for engagement between service providers and their clients, were raised in the consultation.

The stakeholders described a quality interpersonal relationship in various ways, highlighting many aspects of the attitudes of staff and providers that impact on people when they meet with their service provider.

Sub-theme 2.1   **Understanding and empathetic relationships**

Views of people using the services

For people using the services, the experience of the relationship is critical in its own right and is not secondary to the treatment or care offered within the relationship. Professionals need an understanding of people's emotional needs – "*less clinical, more empathetic*" - and a strong awareness of the impact that their approach and demeanour have on people.

The characteristics of a healing relationship were described in different, but connected ways. People spoke especially about the need for understanding, sympathetic, caring relationships. They referred to the need to feel comfortable, and at ease. ***There should be no sense of "being judged or blamed"*** for their difficulties. Friendliness, flexibility and reassurance help people using the service to have a good experience in their interaction with their service provider, as well as a relaxed atmosphere.

The relationships should be such that trust and confidence in the service provider can develop. Linked to this was the need for honesty, openness and integrity in the relationship.

The first contact with the service provider should be handled sensitively, confidently and professionally. The role of the receptionist is particularly important at the first contact – "*a smile is a great help*".

Views of families, parents and carers

Families referred to the importance of **'humanising the service'.** Having an understanding and compassionate engagement with their family generated many stories of quality experiences of the mental health services. Compatibility with the service provider is important, as well as a sympathetic and patient approach.

Families underlined the need for understanding relationships with all staff with whom the person with a mental health problem comes in contact. The relationship with the community mental health nurse was mentioned, but also the need for positive contacts with receptionists and cleaning staff.

An indicator of the relationship is how people with mental health problems are spoken to and how they are listened to. Listening validates concerns and builds confidence and trust. It is not enough to listen – people need to be believed, particularly about the effects of treatment and a genuine effort made to understand what the person wants to convey about their illness. A personalised service and a genuine interest in the individual are further marks of a quality relationship.

Views of service providers

The quality of communication was seen as crucial to the relationship. Open and informal lines of communication between the main service provider and the person with a mental health problem will facilitate the relationship. Services need to be based on needs-led, personalised interventions where the patient's needs are at the centre of planning, and where individual differences are respected.

People using the services need open-ended time with the service provider, rather than time-limited meetings, and dedicated time for each client with professional staff.

Service providers need to demonstrate cultural sensitivity, and sensitivity to language needs. Services should be culturally competent. Service providers should also respect the ways in which people want to use language – for example, they may want to use the language of emotional health, rather than mental health.

Views of people using the service

The individual who is availing of the mental health service should be treated with respect and their sense of their own dignity should be protected and enhanced by the experience of receiving the service. Service users see a need to be respected as customers and given individual attention.

People want to have a sense of being regarded as a 'normal person', and accepted as a person on an equal basis with the provider. People with addictions want to be treated 'humanely'.

People using the service described behaviours that tend to undermine their dignity and signal a lack of respect. Some spoke about the importance of not being "*talked down to*" and not being related to "*from a superior educational point of view*" or in what feels like a condescending manner. People want to be spoken to directly, with eye contact. "*Corridor consultations*" were viewed as disrespectful. For deaf people in particular, service providers need to make sure that they talk directly to the person.

GPs need to understand and be sensitive to deaf culture. Elderly people, especially those in long-stay facilities, should be treated respectfully. Children may find the style of adult questioning, and questioning of families, alienating.

The belief that what passes between the person using the service and the service provider will be treated in confidence was another dimension of a respectful relationship mentioned by service users.

Finally, people using the service spoke about **the need to be listened to as key to a respectful service**. The readiness of professionals to listen was a characteristic of many of the stories told about positive and successful engagements with the mental health services.

Views of families, parents and carers

Families referred to the importance of an ethos of respect from all staff, including non-medical staff, in a quality service. There was a concern about the status of the individual and how they are perceived by staff. **No stigma should be attached to the person with mental illness.** They should be treated in the same way as you would treat people with any other illness, or in any other hospital. Poor people should not be treated less well than rich people. Non-stigmatising service delivery is essential, so that people are not further excluded from the mainstream of society.

There was a view that people should have a choice about the gender of the nurse looking after them, especially for bathing purposes.

People using the services expect that their personal circumstances will be kept confidential. They also want privacy, especially for interviews.

As with people using the service, families believe that time with the provider makes it possible to develop the kind of relationships of trust that people want – *"ten to fifteen minutes once a week does not inspire confidence that correct conclusions can be drawn"*. Regular contact, at frequent intervals, is needed for a quality service, according to families.

Views of service providers

A client-centred culture, based on respectful attitudes on the part of all staff, underpins a quality service, in the view of providers. This culture should extend to all staff who engage with people using the service, including staff escorting people to hospital. People need non-judgemental relationships, which accord equality of status to the client, and in which there is a mutuality of respect, with the service user regarded and treated as a customer. Empathetic listening should allow the person to speak, and should require the provider to act on what they hear.

Transparent decision-making, access for people to their files, and confidentiality were seen as further elements of service delivery likely to generate relationships of respect and trust.

The issue of informed consent was raised. Referrals may be made without the person's knowledge, and they may be telephoned by the service provider, not knowing that they have been referred.

The provision of privacy, and a confidential service, would be a mark of quality from service providers' perspective. There was a view that people who use mental health services should be made aware of the code of ethics of the providers, and their qualifications.

Views of organisations with an interest in mental health

These organisations expressed broadly similar views to other stakeholders. They emphasised the importance of openness and transparency as hall marks of a quality service.

Views of members of the public

Staff should be person-centred, not focused on the perspectives of the organisation, or their own particular profession or discipline. One of the indicators of a respectful service would be an appointment system, where everyone was not given the same appointment time. Good listening is essential, rather than prescribing straight away.

Views of people using the service

The stigma associated with mental illness adds to the unease that people can feel in approaching services. ***For children and young people, normalising the use of the service is especially important.*** Children need to feel understood. They need to feel that being sad or happy are normal feelings. The business of children being, or feeling, labelled by their engagement with the services should be understood and addressed by service providers.

The stigma associated with using the services may create additional barriers for people from different cultural backgrounds. Service providers need to understand these cultural contexts, and take account of them.

Views of service providers

Service providers identified some of the ways in which services need to be organised and managed in order to facilitate healing relationships. Staff need an awareness of the ways in which they themselves can hold stigmatising views. The need for non-stigmatising and anonymous models of service delivery was mentioned in this context. The integration of mental health services into medical centres at local level, and the presence of a psychiatric nurse in GP clinics were given as examples.

Views of organisations with an interest in mental health

These organisations expressed broadly similar views to other stakeholders. They highlighted the importance of non-stigmatising forms of service delivery, and of the quality of communication between professionals and the service provider.

Views of members of the public

Members of the public believe that people with mental health problems need understanding and respect, and help to overcome the stigma associated with mental illness. Teenagers in particular need a normalised service that does not stigmatise them, and where it is 'ok' to attend.

A good telephone manner and a good 'bedside manner' would be important to people. The GP in particular was mentioned as someone who needs to be supportive and understanding towards people who come with mental health problems.

The language around mental illness should be used with sensitivity and in a non-stigmatising way – ***"do not talk about people 'suffering from' mental illness"***.

An empowering approach to service delivery is beneficial to both people using the service and those providing them

It is not enough that the relationships between service users and service providers are respectful, understanding and caring. A quality service will empower the people who use the mental health services. It will accord them equality of status within the relationship, enable them to take as much responsibility for their own health and well-being as they can take, and provide them with the supports they need to maximise autonomy, choice, and self-determination. An empowering relationship between the person using a mental health service and those providing it will need to be supported by mechanisms like information provision, complaints procedures, advocacy systems, and training for both providers and service users.

These views were widely shared among all stakeholders. *Service providers, in particular, emphasised the need for a culture of empowerment and for organisational mechanisms to develop that culture.*

According to stakeholders, mechanisms for empowerment are needed that go beyond the level of individual service users. Organisational arrangements should be in place for giving service users and families a say in policy and governance. This will help to embed the culture of partnership and participation.

The main facets of quality in an empowering approach to service delivery include

- Knowledge and information to support involvement

- Partnership in planning, review and decision-making

- Choice, rights and informed consent

- Access to peer support

- Mechanisms for participation (complaints procedures, advocacy, and structures for influencing policy)

Views of people using the services

Knowledge and information about all aspects of one's own mental health problem are essential if people are to participate well in their recovery programme, in the view of service users.

People want to understand the nature of their illness, how it is likely to progress and how it will affect their lives. They want to understand the prognosis for recovery. They want to have more information about treatments and their impact, and about medication. In particular, any side effects of medication must be explained. Doctors should not withhold information because they assume people will not understand. There was a view that patients should be able to report side effects of medication directly to the Irish Medicines Board.

People need advice about how they themselves can help to manage their own condition, and to know where to go when they need this advice. This means being able to recognise and anticipate problems, and to know what to do if there are warning signs that their health is disimproving or relapsing. People want to be enabled to take more responsibility for their lives and minimise dependence on the services. Treatment and medication should be explained in clear, jargon-free language.

People using services want to have control over their own care and be part of decision-making about their recovery plan – *"to be actively involved in decision-making, rather than being instructed"*. Joint decision-making will mean that nothing is decided without the knowledge and informed consent of the individual. A documented programme of recovery for each person using the mental health services should be developed in collaboration with the service user, and agreed by both parties as soon as the service user has the capacity to do so.

Having choice is very important - choice of professional and choice of service. Information about treatment options is essential if people are to have choices. A customer service ethos should prevail in the relationship.

Service users want access to complaints processes and to have those complaints taken seriously. They want to be able to question a diagnosis. In a quality service, they would have access to independent advice, and access to their own records. Having access to peer support and peer groups is also an important part of the recovery process.

Both individual service users and service user groups identified the need for formal mechanisms through which people using services can be partners with providers both at an individual level and collectively. The mechanisms mentioned were:

- Access to a full range of advocacy services, including peer advocates, and training for self-advocacy

- Information provision to each service user by the mental health provider about the range of voluntary sector services and their potential benefits

- Linkages between mental health teams and local support groups as standard practice

- Local support groups involved in both service planning and service delivery

Some groups need particular supports in order to engage with service providers in a manner that enhances independence and possibilities for empowerment. Service providers should have access to deaf-friendly ways of communicating, and to interpreters. They should have the readiness to involve a deaf person in the planning of their own recovery programme. At a broader level, deaf mentors should be available to raise awareness in schools and colleges and families of deaf people should have access to education in Irish Sign Language.

For refugees and asylum seekers, or indeed for any person who may have difficulty with the complex language that can be used in relation to diagnosis, medication and prognosis, service providers should ensure that simple, accessible information is provided and that interpreters are available. In clinics and centres, non-verbal signage should be provided, as well as language-based signs.

At a broader level, refugee support groups and organisations should be involved in disseminating information about mental health and mental health services in refugee centres. Similarly, organisations supporting homeless people should be invited to get involved in communicating information about mental health services to people who are homeless.

Children and young people have the same expectations as adults that they will be involved and treated as purchasers of services. Awareness among service providers of young people's issues should be improved. Those who are inviting young people to be referred to mental health services should be knowledgeable about those services, and should prepare the young person and the family for using and understanding the service.

Children and young people should have options and choices, and the right to exercise choice. For example, they may opt to work with a counsellor or a nurse. Access to supportive complaints procedures, and to an advocate, is particularly important for children and young people.

Children and young people too should have ways of influencing policy developments. There was a view that this is best done through their own representative groups rather than through participation in adult forums.

Views of families, parents and carers

The views of families, parents and carers mirrored the views of people using the service very closely. They too underlined the need for access to knowledge and accurate, honest information to enable people to play a greater part in their own management and recovery programme. They also emphasised the need for options and choice, and mechanisms to support this level of empowerment. On the topic of medication in particular, clear information about dosages and compliance is essential.

People should know what to expect from the service from first contact through discharge and follow-up. They should have a view and that view should be valued. The need for choice of service and choice of provider is hampered, in the view of some families, by the catchment area system.

Families, parents and carers highlighted the value and importance of their own role in the recovery process and the need for service providers to facilitate that role by giving information and explanations to both the family and the individual. Views about the importance of education for families in helping and supporting their family members are discussed in more detail in Chapter 4.

Families referred to the need for a human rights-based approach to service provision, though the implications of this in terms of service delivery was not developed in any detail. *Families also see group support and group meetings as an important element of an empowering approach to recovery,* and they believe that people using the services should have access to formal advocacy systems.

Views of service providers

In the view of service providers, *a quality mental health service will promote autonomy and maximise choices.* Clear information on pathways into, through and out of the services is essential for people using the services. People using the services should be consulted, involved and offered choices – choices in relation to service location, the professionals delivering the service, and the treatment. The lack of choice was seen as a barrier to improvements in service quality. Where the person's choice is not feasible, clear explanations should be given as to the reasons.

Service providers should engage people in a partnership approach, in which needs are identified and decisions made in collaboration with the person using the service. People should be given realistic expectations in order to avoid frustrations. *Families, parents and carers should be acknowledged as key members of the service delivery team,* and there should be regular consultation with them, subject to the constraints of client confidentiality. Care plans should be developed for the person using the service, with family and friends, the key worker and other relevant professionals involved in discharge planning.

For people attending sheltered workshops, the question of employee rights and pay should be looked at as part of the delivery of a quality service.

Service providers focused more strongly than other groups on the mechanisms that are needed to enable them to offer an empowering model of service. Empowered staff, who are themselves listened to, was mentioned as a prerequisite. Policies and procedures are needed to embed an empowering ethos in the services. Those policies should be transparent, and people (staff and service users) should be provided with information about them.

Those using the services should inform the service philosophy. Children and young people and their families, in particular, should help to shape the ethos of their services, and children should have access to independent advocacy services. There was a proposal to the effect that high quality empowerment and choice would be more feasible if funding were linked to individual need.

In a quality service, mechanisms are needed for involving those who use the service in all aspects of the design, delivery and monitoring of services, and in all consultative groups. There was a suggestion that consideration should be given to paying service users for their involvement in service planning at the organisational level. People should be made aware of complaints procedures. Service review mechanisms that include feedback about services are an integral part of an empowering model of service provision. The need for a patient's charter was also raised.

Formal links are needed with voluntary sector organisations, and those organisations should have ways of participating in policy development, implementation and evaluation.

The need for consultant psychiatrists to engage, in equal partnership, with agencies providing services to people with learning disabilities, was raised.

Views of organisations with an interest in mental health

Organisations with an interest in mental health shared the views of all other stakeholders in relation to the need for an empowering approach as a key element of a quality service.

These organisations highlighted the importance of access to information. With regard to choice, people using services should be able to challenge decisions about their treatment. Accessible complaints procedures, both formal and informal, are essential, but it was felt that the absence of a choice of doctor inhibits people from complaining, for fear of repercussions or fear of being treated differently. A complaints officer should be available, it was felt, who would act as a 'buffer' against repercussions.

Views of members of the public

Members of the public highlighted **the need for choice of service.** When people give feedback about how medication is affecting them, or if they want to cut down on medication, they should be listened to. If doctors are to give people the ability to manage their medication, they need to see them every week.

Information provision is essential if people are to have real choice, but information must be given in a way that makes it accessible – "*don't just hand over a leaflet – discuss it*". When doctors know more than the patient about the patient's condition, this is a kind of control.

Complaints procedures should "make it safe to speak". People should be able to complain to an independent body, and complaints should be acted upon and followed up.

A quality environment, respecting the dignity of the individual and the family, will result in a more positive experience

Not surprisingly, stakeholders see the quality of the physical surroundings as having a strong impact on those using mental health services and on their recovery process. This was the view of all stakeholders. Part of the requirement of a quality service is to provide settings and surroundings that respect the dignity of the individual, ensure basic comforts, meet needs, guarantee an acceptable level of privacy, and, at least, equate with the physical and accommodation standards in other health services.

The aspects of a quality environment that impact on people's experience of a quality service spanned:

- The standard of physical buildings

- The appropriateness of the physical facilities and their 'fit' with the needs of particular groups

- The range of services and activities available (particularly in long-stay settings)

- The quality of food and nutrition provided

Views of people using the services

Services should be provided in a healing environment, according to people using mental health services. *Buildings should be clean, tidy and well maintained. Rooms should be bright and well decorated.*

The expectations people have for a quality environment vary according to the location. In a hostel setting, a home-like atmosphere would improve quality of life. Facilities that enhance independence (an example given was access to tea-making facilities rather than a tea dispensing machine or tea served at fixed times) were mentioned, as well as recreation facilities other than television.

The quality of waiting rooms could also be improved, particularly in the light of extended waiting times for out-patient clinics. Reference was made to relatively small matters that result in poor quality experience in waiting rooms, such as the television fixed on one station, and the stock of women's magazines but no reading material for men.

In the case of hospitals, people named bright wards, privacy and smaller rooms rather than large wards, as elements of a quality environment, as well as having ways of keeping property safe. Families should have access to a coffee shop. Fresh, nutritious food should be available to patients.

The environment should be appropriate to those using the services. The need for accommodation and environments suited to the needs of children was stressed. Children and young people need a safe environment. Minimum standards for this should be put in place, as for other areas of standards.

For people who are deaf, the environment must be deaf friendly, with basic communication aids in place, such as signs at reception areas.

Views of families, parents and carers

The psychological impact of the physical surroundings was captured by families in references to the ***need for peaceful, friendly and safe environments that are less sterile and less intimidating.*** They particularly identified the need for an appropriate and respectful environment in long stay services.

Views of service providers

Service providers cited the need for well-maintained surroundings and a non-threatening environment, as well as a proper and respectful working environment for staff.

Providers also highlighted the need for a welcoming environment, particularly in admissions areas, and wheelchair accessibility. A safe environment is an element of quality, in their view. Personal comforts for patients, such as appropriate clothing, protect people's dignity.

In relation to matching settings to the needs of particular client groups, service providers made reference to the need for a dedicated in-patient facility for people with learning difficulties and mental illness, as part of a quality service for them.

Buildings for mental health services should be of a similar standard to other health services. The suitability of transport arrangements should be part of the consideration of a quality service.

Views of organisations with an interest in mental health

While the environment has less impact on service quality than the attributes of those providing services, nonetheless, many environments are unsuitable and fall short of what is needed to give a good quality experience and a safe environment to those using the services.

Views of members of the public

Healthy buildings and healthy food would be available in a quality service, in the view of members of the public.

Theme 5

Easy access to services is key to a quality service

The sub-themes, relating to this theme, identified during the consultation, include:

5.1 *Information*

5.2 *Equitable access and ease of access*

5.3 *Flexible services*

The requirements for quality in mental health services, as in other health services, include access to the service in the first instance. All stakeholders share the view that ***quality and access cannot be separated.***

Access should be equitable. The service should be there when people need it and where they need it. Having information about where to go and how to find what you need is a basic access requirement, but, even before that, people must know where to get that information.

The systems for managing access such as referral paths, geographical units of service, and eligibility systems should facilitate the person, as well as facilitating ease of administration.

The core elements of a high quality service, from the point of view of access, include all of the following:

*   Information about services

*   Equitable access

*   Ease of access

*   Flexible, user-centred availability

Sub-theme 5.1 **Information**

Views of people using the services

People using mental health services need precise information about where to get those services. In particular, they ***need information about where to go for their first contact with mental health services.*** Literature should be widely displayed. A directory of mental health services, which would also explain what the different levels of service do, would be helpful for people using the services and families.

There is also a need for information at critical points in the recovery path. For example, people wanting to get back to work or training, and in particular people who may have lost their jobs, need information suited to their needs at that time.

Ways of delivering this information include a comprehensive website for the public about mental health services. The information should be provided in a manner that is accessible to people who have literacy problems.

Information must be delivered in ways that are accessible to people from minority groups including refugees and asylum seekers. Interpreting services are limited and expensive. The ability to speak English does not necessarily mean that people can read the language.

Views of families, parents and carers

For 'first-time' users of mental health services, a help line staffed by highly trained and knowledgeable staff who could answer queries from the public would be of great assistance. Not knowing where to go or what to do when a family member is ill was seen as a big difficulty for families. People should be told where to go next, if the service they approach initially cannot help their family member. GP surgeries and citizen's advice bureaux should distribute information to the public on all aspects of mental health and mental health services, including benefits, support groups, and housing options.

Sub-theme 5.2 **Equitable access and ease of access**

Views of people using the services

People want equitable care. The cost of services should not stop people from getting the help they need. People using the service see this as meaning that you do not access just any service, but **you get the service that is right for you, irrespective of cost.** There was a view that prescribed medication should be free and that access to services such as counselling and alternative therapies should also be free - "*you should not have to get what you need at your own expense*".

There was a perception that people availing of private mental health services have access to a wider range of treatment options, and are more likely to be treated as customers than people using public services.

Access to mental health services for people in rural areas should be of an equal standard to services in urban areas, and lack of transport impacts on this. Access should not be affected by one's culture.

People do not want to have to spend long periods on waiting lists for services. They do not want to spend long periods in waiting rooms at outpatient clinics. They would like better queuing systems.

In a quality service, it should be possible to access services quickly in a crisis, and without appointments at times of need. People wish to have more time with the psychiatrist and to see him/her more often – *"seeing the psychiatrist for 15 minutes every three months"* – a theme that also arose in the context of respectful services. The view was that people, especially people who are homeless, or who have addiction problems, need more time to discuss problems.

People should have appropriate access at primary care level - *"not everyone needs to see a psychiatrist"*.

In the view of groups and organisations working with children and young people, children, in particular, need a readily available service. Direct access to child guidance clinics should be possible, rather than having to go through a GP. This would remove what is seen as a barrier to ready access. Different channels and points of entry to services are needed for children and young people.

Speedy access in a crisis is seen as especially significant for children. The example given was that of a four-year old child waiting 13 months for access. User friendly information directed at children and young people themselves should be provided.

There was a view that people who have behavioural problems, personality disorders, or dual diagnosis, such as addiction and mental illness, are being restricted from accessing services by the legislative definitions of mental illness currently used to determine eligibility for services.

The catchment area system of managing referrals is seen as particularly disadvantageous in terms of equality of access for homeless people. For some vulnerable groups who are at risk of offending, timely intervention is especially important, in order to ensure that they do not compound their problems by getting into difficulties with the law.

According to the National Traveller Health Strategy (2002 - 2005), the take-up of mental health services by Travellers is believed to be low, probably on account of a combination of inappropriate provision and a lack of awareness or confidence among Travellers in relation to services.

Views of families, parents and carers

In addition to the elements of an accessible service identified by people who use the services, families would like clear referral systems and pathways. Routes other than the GP route were suggested, for example access through a public health nurse who could refer without appointments. There should be a minimum of 'hassle' and bureaucracy around admissions and self-referral to a psychiatrist should be possible.

For people living in rural areas, the difficulty of travelling long distances to meet tight appointment deadlines was seen as a problem that could be addressed by having locally based services.

There was a view that people with mental health problems should not have to wait in A&E departments of general hospitals, or that a psychiatric nurse should be on the staff of A&E departments.

Some families see access for people with learning difficulties and mental health problems as a particular problem. They cited difficulties in getting admission to psychiatric hospitals for a family member with this dual diagnosis.

Views of service providers

The views of service providers in relation to access focused mainly on equity, flexibility and ease of access, as well as access for minority groups and people in rural areas. Equity of access for people with learning disability and mental illness is seen as particularly problematic. Ease of access, in the view of service providers, helps to challenge the stigma associated with mental illness.

Service providers focused on some of the 'system' issues that need to be addressed in a quality service, in relation to access. Concern was expressed that any 'address-based' service will restrict choice for people using the services. The length of the 'referral chain' between GP contact and meeting with a specialist team was seen as a problem. *People should be seen quickly following GP referral.*

Particular models of service are also seen as limiting access. For example, people must experience significant levels of mental illness before they can get access to a service.

Intake meetings or systems to deal with referrals and to co-ordinate the referral process would smooth access. Clear mechanisms are needed to 'fast-track' people in acute situations. Emergency services for people who deliberately self-harm and people who are actively psychotic are a critical element of an accessible service.

To smooth access, admissions processes should begin in the home. There needs to be a streamlining of the 'handover' process at the point where ambulance crews bring a person for admission to hospital.

Helpline services should be available in each Health Board area. Priority should be given to the most vulnerable people to optimise scarce resources. One view was that the priority setting process should exclude people whose difficulties can be seen as social problems rather than mental illness.

One matter related to access raised only by service providers is the need to have good ways of exiting services as well as good ways of entry.

Views of organisations with an interest in mental health

Organisations with an interest in mental health services stressed the need for consistency of service in all areas across the country and among providers, as well as equality of access for people from rural areas with people in urban areas.

The problems for people with an unclear diagnosis, who may fall between providers were highlighted, as well as access problems that arise if service providers "*pick and choose*" as to the kinds of mental health problem they will address.

People need knowledge and understanding of what services are in place and how these link with the work of the Mental Health Commission in relation to service quality. Information needs in relation to mental health need to be brought to the attention of Comhairle. People need information about the role and work of the voluntary and community sector.

Views of members of the public

Information about different providers in an area would be of great help to the public, as well as information about how to access a service. People do not know if they can go directly to the health centre or whether they have to see a GP. There was a view that access to certain treatments like alternative therapies are restricted if the GP is not aware of the options.

Sub-theme 5.3 **Flexible services**

Views of people using the services

People using mental health services want many kinds of flexibility in a quality service. ***Opening times suited to people's needs or personal situation was an important element of a flexible service.*** Services should be available 24 hours a day and seven days a week, all year round, particularly to ensure that they could be accessed in emergency situations. Drop-in centres should be available seven days a week. People would also like to have the option of a telephone consultation with their psychiatrist.

Views of families, parents and carers

Families, parents and carers see the availability of home-based and outreach services as an important aspect of a flexible service. A crisis response should be there for a person in immediate danger of self-harm, or who are a danger to others. People with a medical card should have access to the full range of health professionals.

Views of members of the public

Locally-based services, longer opening hours for services, including weekend services, outreach services, shorter waiting lists, and affordable services were the areas where members of the public see scope for improvement in the quality of access to mental health services. People should not have to make up excuses to get off work to attend clinics with privacy and confidentiality.

Theme 6

Receiving a skilful service and high standards of care is extremely important to people using mental health services

High standards of professional care and treatment are an important element of a quality service. This dimension of quality was a stronger theme for families, parents and carers and for people using mental health services, than for other groups, though all groups made reference to it. In the case of service providers, their focus on quality of care and treatment is captured more fully in their views on mechanisms for quality assurance, and on training and development.

The quality of the relationships between those using the services and the providers is, of course, a critical feature of a skilful service and one that was strongly evident in the feedback as outlined separately under theme 3.2. It is interesting to note that the focus on the *quality* of actual treatment or care, and the outcomes of that care, was less prominent in the consultation feedback than material dealing with the *quantity* and availability of services, or the relationships experienced in the course of service provision.

The main elements of quality noted in relation to this theme were the need for people to experience quality care to international standards of best practice, the quality of diagnosis and prescribing, and the need for outcome focused interventions. All stakeholders emphasised the importance of these in a quality service.

Views of people using the services

Service users expect a high standard of care and professionalism in a quality service, reflecting best current thinking in the management of mental health and mental illness. This is seen as depending in large measure on the skills of the providers, both clinical and managerial.

A recovery focused approach to treatment and support/care is important for people using mental health services. They believe *the goal must be improvement in their quality of life, the possibility of being well and staying well, to be able to build a normal lifestyle outside the institution, take responsibility, and hold down a job if possible.* Adoption of the principle of recovery will require a shift away from ideas like 'cure' and 'treatment' and a greater emphasis on ideas such as self-management and facilitation.

Having confidence in the medication prescribed is an important aspect of quality. They want to know that the medication is based on up-to-date knowledge of what is available. A further dimension of prescribing that is important to people using the services is the need for doctors to attend fully to the side effects of medication, and for medication to be supervised and checked regularly.

For some, the question of standards of quality care is also one of comparisons. They want to be able to expect the same quality of care whether they are in a public or a private mental health service, and to expect similar standards in mental health services as they could expect in general hospitals.

Provision for children and young people raised particular quality issues. Hospitalisation needs to be handled well, treatment should be age appropriate, and professionals giving services should be skilled in delivering the kinds of evidence-based interventions that are appropriate for children. Models of service delivery used should be known to be effective for a child population. These aspects of service quality were raised too in relation to children and young people with learning disability and mental health problems.

For people who are deaf, the quality of service is closely linked to the availability of people who can communicate effectively with them. The availability of a social worker who is deaf would address this need in some measure. There was also a view that closer networking is needed between the generalist psychiatrist giving a service to a deaf person, and a psychiatrist with specialised experience of working with deaf people.

For people with alcohol and other addictions, one additional concern was that a quality service should be available to them if they should be in prison.

Health checks for refugees and asylum seeking adults should include a mental health assessment. For this group, it was difficult to separate a consideration of a skilful service from the concerns about the overall levels of mental health service provision in Direct Provision Centres, and the level of availability of mental health services for this group outside of Dublin.

Views of families, parents and carers

The views of families, parents and carers were very similar to those of people using the services. They expect high standards of recovery-focused professional care for their family member from all the people involved in their service provision and at all stages in the process.

Professionals should be aware of modern thinking worldwide, and up to date with the advantages of a wide range of approaches. Networking among professionals would enable this to happen. There was a view that the gap in availability in Ireland, compared to the UK, of people with specialist expertise in mental health dimensions of conditions such as acquired brain injury and ADHD is seriously detrimental to people with those conditions. The model of service delivery for people with these conditions would also have to be different from the general model of mental health service provision, if it is to deliver a skilful quality service.

A skilful service from GPs was seen to be particularly important, and to depend in some measure, at least, on their knowledge of local services, and their willingness to refer on, as well as on their own expertise in this area.

Diagnosis should be broadly based, including psychological assessment where appropriate, and should help the person to develop a good insight into their situation. There was a view that families should be involved in the diagnostic process, giving their experience. The diagnosis should be an in-depth process that probes for a full understanding of the person's circumstances. Physical health should be assessed as well as mental health at the point of admission to hospital, as part of the diagnostic process.

While families noted the importance of appropriate, well-supervised and effective medication in a quality service, and 'optimal', as distinct from 'maintenance' treatment, the readiness to move to other forms of support after a person's condition has stabilised, was also raised, together with the need for systematic treatment reviews to ensure continued effectiveness of treatment.

Views of service providers

As noted earlier, the views of service providers in relation to the quality of a skilful service overlaps with extensive views about training and development needs and mechanisms for ensuring high quality services. This material is treated more fully in Chapter 5 of this report.

According to service providers, a skilful service will mean a commitment on the part of providers to standards of excellence, adherence to codes of ethics, accredited therapists and high standards.

In the matter of diagnosis, there was a view that diagnosis should include routine conducting of psycho-social assessments in the case of people causing self-harm, to discover any underlying social or psychological influences. Diagnosis should reflect a holistic approach to meeting needs.

A skilful service is intrinsically linked to an appropriate service, in the view of service providers. *Appropriate referral and service appropriate to need are key dimensions of a skilful service, particularly in the case of people with needs associated with dual diagnoses.*

An outcome-focused approach will aim to support the individual towards mature, independent functioning and responsible compliance, alongside reduced reliance on medication as far as possible.

4 What constitutes a quality service for families, parents and carers?

"I believe it is important, when attempting to offer a quality service, that the views of the family of the patient are held in the highest regard ... that they are consulted and informed about all drugs and therapies, where possible, and that they take an active part in the support of the patient."

[person using/has used mental health services]

"Many families are frightened by their family member returning from hospital. They feel alone, isolated from the rest of the community and anxious for their own safety and that of the patient."

[organisation]

"Support for families is often a neglected area. Having a family member who is diagnosed with a mental health difficulty can be very distressing for all concerned, not just the individual with the diagnosis. There may be guilt, shame, anger, anxiety and a range of other emotions which require support and assistance to deal with. Family members need to be allowed to express these emotions and be provided with support and assistance to deal with them."

[organisation]

A quality service is one where ... "As a carer more information [is available] from one point, as opposed to resorting to trekking around a number of service centres to get information."

[not attributable]

"I have heard so many [families] complaining, they are completely brushed aside by the psychiatrist and consequently by his/her team. I had personal experience of this. By the nature of the illness, the patient sometimes gives a distorted picture. The carer and family see a more objective picture and know the true needs of the patient – they must be listened to."

[family member/carer]

Introduction

What constitutes a quality service for families, parents and carers?

Themes emerging from the consultation

7 Families, parents and carers need to be empowered as team members, receiving information and advice, as appropriate	8 Effective family support services need to be in place to reflect the important role families, parents and carers play in a person's healing	9 Families parents and carers need to experience understanding, empathy and respect

Families, parents and carers of people using mental health services have strong expectations about service quality for their family members. They also have needs in their own right, since a person's illness may have profound effects for the family, and place new kinds of pressures on them.

It is not always easy to separate what families see as their own needs from what they want for their family member. The pain and frustration they feel when they cannot help the person, or when someone will not co-operate with service providers, was very evident in submissions and workshop discussions. Their need for information and advice is bound up with their carer role and their wish to support the person who is experiencing difficulty. Follow-up and support for a person using the service following discharge from hospital is a shared need – to enable both the individual and their families or carers to cope well and help each other.

Families need a range of support services for themselves at various stages in their family member's illness and recovery process. Like service users, they expect understanding and empathy, and a respectful service. They want to be part of a solution-focused approach to recovery, and to play a constructive part in the team aiding the person who is experiencing mental health problems.

Other stakeholders are supportive of these expectations. Service providers, in particular, acknowledge the part that families can and should be enabled to play, and the importance of empowering them for this role.

There were clear differences of view between families and service users about the level of involvement that families can legitimately expect to have in relation to knowledge about the person's illness, information about treatment, planning and decision-making.

In summary, three key themes emerged from the consultation process in relation to what constitutes a quality service for families, parents and carers. These themes were emphasised by all of the different stakeholder groups during the consultation:

- Families, parents and carers need to be empowered as team members, receiving information and advice as appropriate

- Effective family support services need to be in place to reflect the important role families, parents and carers play in a person's healing

- As with people who use mental health services, families, parents and carers need to experience understanding, empathy and respect

The views of each of the different stakeholder groups, expressed during the consultation in relation to each theme, are described in the rest of this chapter. As explained in relation to Chapter 3, Prospectus sought to reflect the diversity of views held by the different stakeholders and to capture all of the suggestions made (whether they were made by one or a large number of stakeholders). Where a specific stakeholder group is not mentioned under a given theme, this means that the stakeholder group did not explicitly refer to this theme during the consultation.

Families, parents and carers need to be empowered as team members, receiving information and advice as appropriate

Views of families, parents and carers

Families highlighted the provision of information and advice as their most pressing need from a quality service. *In the first instance, they need factual information about what services are available, how the services work, and how to access them, especially in a crisis.* Information about support groups for carers, workshops about mental illness run by health boards, and peer support groups where people can exchange views were found by families to be particularly helpful to them. Families would like to be able to influence organisation policies, through membership of boards or working groups.

Once a family member is 'in the system', parents and carers believe they should be regarded by professionals as part of the team. They have valuable insights and experience they can bring to bear on diagnosis, decision-making, choice of treatment options and recovery planning. They want to be able to access the doctor or psychiatrist, and engage in dialogue with them where this is appropriate – *"how can we understand or help when we don't know?"*. One of the priorities for families is to have peace of mind, and to be satisfied that their family member is receiving high quality care.

In order to help their family member, particularly when that person is living at home, families would like to be offered information about appointments, to be aware of medication and side effects, dosages and compliance requirements, expected side effects and prognosis. Families would like guidance as to how they can pro-actively contribute to the recovery plan.

It was noted that a change in the status of a service user's status from 'involuntary' to 'voluntary' patient can result in a sudden end to communication with families.

Families accept the need for client confidentiality, but express a great deal of concern about its impact and about the way providers operate the provision. Essential information, for example in relation to discharge planning, may be withheld from families on grounds of client confidentiality. On the other hand, a skilful professional can help a person to understand the benefits of sharing information with their family. There was a view that this matter must be examined more fully, with a view to ensuring that families are allowed to discuss aspects of their family member's illness or treatment when this is in the person's best interests. Service providers also see this issue as difficult and contentious.

General information about a treatment process should be available to the family, which would not compromise confidentiality but would 'normalise' the process for them.

Families need access to complaints procedures. The fear of complaining was raised, on account of the autonomy of the provider. Advocacy services are needed by families as well as service users.

Views of people using the services

Families need a clear understanding of the mental health legislation. They may need help with forms, if reading is a problem, and how to find their way through the system.

People using the services caution about the damage that can be caused to family relationships if families take actions that are not acceptable to the person who is ill. *Clear boundaries are needed around family involvement, and communication between families and providers must be in line with the wishes of the person using the service.* The rights and choices of young people over eighteen need clarification.

Families of children using mental health services must be respected as partners with professionals, with valuable knowledge to share. The parents need clear information about treatment processes, in readily understood language. They should know how to recognise the early warning signs of difficulty and how to respond. Families of children with autism should be given information on where to go for services. In the case of young people at school, teachers also need to know how to recognise signs of distress or to deal with young people's fears. Families also need help from school guidance and counselling services.

The hearing families of deaf people with no sign language have difficulty communicating and can tend to rely on institutional care unnecessarily as a result. Good communication training systems for such families are needed to address this issue.

Views of service providers

Service providers felt that in a quality service, families should have ways of participating in service evaluation and in the planning of future service development to achieve continuous improvement in resource utilisation. There was also a view that families should participate in looking at the relevance of initiatives and best practice models.

Views of organisations with an interest in mental health

Families need particular guidance about how to respond when a potentially violent person returns home. This is particularly the case for elderly parents or one-parent families.

Accurate, unbiased information should be given, in a way that takes account of possible literacy problems. Families should be fully involved in decisions about discharge, and given timely information to ensure readiness, planning and preparation.

Views of members of the public

Members of the public said that families should be involved and consulted, and should be able to question the medical profession. Professionals should 'lift the veil' on mental illness for the family, and hold the family in high regard.

Effective family support services need to be in place to reflect the important role families, parents and carers play in a person's healing

Views of families, parents and carers

Families need support at every stage in the person's illness and recovery process. In particular *they highlighted the need for counselling and therapy to help them to deal with pressures on their own mental health, arising from stress and anxiety.* Family therapy is needed to help to rebuild family relationships, and to give support to siblings of the person who is ill.

Families need access to respite services, a key worker for the family, access to a help line or other support in crisis situations (such as for families of people who self-harm or are violent), and visits to the family by the community psychiatric nurse.

Families should not be unduly burdened by the need to provide accommodation for an adult relative with mental health problems, and there should not be an undue expectation on the part of providers that siblings can undertake the care of their brother or sister. There was a view that the absence of a housing entitlement for an adult, if the family home is available, is unfair and should be changed. A database for housing planning for mental health services is needed in order to avoid this burden on families.

Views of people using the services

People using mental health services recognise the role that families can play in their recovery plan, and believe that they should have the supports they need for this. They identify the same kinds of support needs as those proposed by families. The role of children as carers for adults needs to be acknowledged and assisted by providers. Voluntary groups play an important part, but should not be expected to take all the responsibility for family support.

Follow-up and outreach services are essential for parents, and was mentioned particularly in the case of people who have addictions. They need a single point of contact, and flexible access to crisis intervention services. A key worker or liaison person linking family, hospital, and other services like the Gardaí would help to ensure a quality service. Families may need help in order to keep the home safe.

The impact of housing legislation on some marginalised groups was emphasised by service user groups. It was indicated that a person must be homeless before they qualify for rent allowance, thus creating an impetus for people to be 'out of home.' Not all people who use the services fit the profile of having a 'typical' family. Providers should help people who are homeless or alone to recreate a substitute family or get community support.

Views of service providers

According to service providers, the continuum of support for families is directly parallel to what people who use the services need – information, empowerment to act as co-therapist and team member, linkages and connections with the team, a seamless service and a key worker, family therapy if needed, and ongoing involvement in the care plan. Service providers should be proactive in offering information and support to families from the first contact with services, and should provide directories of local services for families.

Providers highlighted the need for children of parents who are mentally ill to be given help to understand their parent's illness. Providers also pointed to the need for a home help service for families with a relative who has mental health problems, as part of a quality continuum of support.

Families of asylum seeking and refugee service users, families of Travellers or linguistic minorities need access to culturally competent services alongside their family member.

Views of organisations with an interest in mental health

A higher degree of support is needed where a family member is being treated at home. Peer support, emotional support and therapy, should be available to families in a quality service. Families need to be reassured that the plan of care for the family member goes beyond 'managing' their condition.

Views of members of the public

Families should be able to network with other families in similar circumstances. The support they get from providers should be aimed at avoiding burnout and illness. The hospice model of care might be a good model for mental health services, from a family perspective.

As with people who use mental health services, families, parents and carers need to experience understanding, empathy and respect

Views of families, parents and carers

As was the case with people using the services, *families expect understanding, empathy and "a shoulder to lean on" in a quality service.* They want to be listened to carefully, and have their views respected. They want to be treated as equals with the professionals and be shown respect, being kept up to date with what happens to their relative. An example given was the need for the primary carer to be informed if a relative is moved from one hospital to another, and to be told why.

Views of people using the services

People using the services caution about assuming that all families want to, or can, be involved. Families should not be overburdened or undue expectations placed on them about the level of support they can offer.

Views of service providers

Service providers felt that the uniqueness of the individual family, its strengths and weaknesses, should be understood and respected by service providers, and an individualised service offered. The level of engagement of the family needs to be negotiated, according to service providers. Their expectations should be managed, for example, in relation to the level of contact between the family and the consultant. Expectations about their relative's illness and its progress also need to be managed, in order to avoid frustration and disappointment when a 'miracle cure' is expected. Families need time to assimilate the nature and implications of diagnoses, and the chance to return to get more information and advice. They also need constructive feedback on what they are doing well, and how they can improve support for the family member. Finally, families need family friendly waiting areas and child friendly visiting arrangements.

5 What is needed to deliver a quality mental health service?

"Confidentiality, but also the need to share client information with other members of the team, needs to be negotiated respectfully with service users."

[organisation]

"I think that the most important factor influencing quality of care is the direction and standards set by those at the top of the ladder – if that is good, everything else falls into place and people will work as a team. The whole dynamic of the team falls apart if there is a weak link at the top."

[family member/carer]

"Management … [will make the biggest difference] … doctors are not managers."

[family member/carer]

"The need for a system of national standards which are signed up to by all stakeholders, have authority and political buy-in, are well-resourced and are regularly monitored and evaluated."

[not attributable]

"I felt that a caring mentality on the part of those dealing with me, i.e. psychiatrists, nurses, fellow patients, was the key to the experience being a largely positive one. I felt it was down to the nature of the attitudes of those charged with the task of helping me to recover. There is no substitute for basic respect and genuine care and concern."

[person using/has used mental health services]

"If there is a poor ethos, then even people who are well trained will become 'contaminated' by the prevailing disrespectful attitude. I have witnessed this in other hospitals. All staff, including administrative staff, must have a respectful and helpful approach to patients and their families."

[family member/carer]

"The biggest difference to quality in mental health services will be made by the adoption of a set of principles that link funding to the achievements of quality accreditation and which engage services in self-assessment and continuous improvement."

[person providing a mental health service]

Introduction

What is needed to deliver a quality mental health service?

Themes and sub-themes emerging from the consultation

10 Staff skills, expertise and morale are key influencers in the delivery of a quality mental health service	**11 Systematic evaluation and review of mental health services, underpinned by best practice, will enable providers to deliver quality services**	**12 The right management systems and structures should be put in place to facilitate the development of a quality mental health service**	**13 The external environment, in which the mental health services operate, has an important role to play in developing a quality mental health service**
10.1 Recruitment and retention of staff	11.1 Evidence based codes of practice	12.1 Management structures	13.1 Funding
10.2 Appropriate staffing levels and expertise	11.2 Monitoring and evaluation	12.2 Managing resources	13.2 Public education on mental health issues
10.3 Training and continuous professional development	11.3 Commitment to quality	12.3 Management processes	13.3 Legislation
			13.4 Getting mental health on the political agenda

Four themes emerged from the consultation process in relation to what is needed to deliver a quality mental health service. These themes were emphasised by all of the different stakeholder groups during the consultation:

- Staff skills, expertise and morale are key influencers in the delivery of a quality mental health service

- Systematic evaluation and review of mental health services, underpinned by best practice, will enable providers to deliver quality services

- The right management systems and structures should be put in place to facilitate the development of a quality mental health service

- The external environment, in which the mental health services operate, has an important role to play in developing a quality mental health service.

The views of each of the different stakeholder groups, expressed during the consultation in relation to each theme, are described in the rest of this chapter. For some themes, a number of sub-themes were identified. As explained in relation to Chapters 3 and 4, Prospectus sought to reflect the diversity of views held by the different stakeholders and to capture all of the suggestions made (whether they were made by one or a large number of stakeholders). Where a specific stakeholder group is not mentioned under a given theme or sub-theme, this means that the stakeholder group did not explicitly refer to this theme or sub-theme during the consultation.

Theme 10

Staff skills, expertise and morale are key influencers in the delivery of a quality mental health service

The sub-themes, relating to this theme, identified during the consultation, include:

10.1   *Recruitment and retention of staff*

10.2   *Appropriate staffing levels and expertise*

10.3   *Training and continuous professional development*

As with many service organisations, human resources play a pivotal part in everyday activity. The key message from the consultation was that, above everything else, the staff delivering the mental health service influenced the quality of the experience. Therefore, for providers to deliver a quality service, they must have the right staff in place with the appropriate skills. In addition to this, service providers must recognise the important role staff play by providing training and professional development opportunities to people working in their organisations.

Sub-theme 10.1   **Recruitment and retention of staff**

The stakeholders consulted all agreed that *a rigorous recruitment process is required to attract quality staff to mental health service providers.* The recruitment process should ensure the suitability of the person to the specific challenges of the mental health services. Once recruited, it is important to provide a working environment that will prevent burnout and encourage longevity in the job. Specific recommendations and views on how exactly this would be achieved are cited below. A well thought through retention programme should help to address the challenges organisations face with human resources. There was general consensus across the stakeholders about these key requirements. Specific views expressed by different groups in relation to recruitment and retention of staff are detailed below.

Views of service providers

Service providers shared the views of other stakeholders that employing quality staff is key to the delivery of a quality mental health service. The importance of recruiting well-trained junior doctors was cited as an example. It was felt that the quality of the service delivered is influenced by staff morale and therefore every effort should be made to provide a good working environment. Examples of how this could be achieved included having responsive management, good staff relations and encouraging team building, to help create a workplace where "*staff feel they are treated equally and fairly*". It was also felt that having a mix of age groups working in an organisation was of benefit.

Retention was raised as a big issue by service providers – exit interviews were considered necessary to explore retention problems further. It was felt that a retention programme was needed in all service provider organisations. The lack of continuity due to the six-month rotation of junior doctors, although unavoidable, was mentioned as having an effect on the quality of the service delivered.

A big challenge highlighted was staff burnout and efforts should be made to overcome this. Having "*manageable caseloads*" and effective managerial supervision were ways in which this could be avoided. One service provider stated that workloads should "*not be so big that staff are overworked and errors result*". Flexible working arrangements are another way to provide a more attractive working environment. Examples provided include flexible working hours, family friendly working arrangements and giving staff the choice of where to work.

Views of people using the service

"Select the best" was the message from people using mental health services. Specifically, the recruitment process should involve potential staff being screened and assessed for suitability to the job and ensuring that s/he is a "*person of integrity*". The importance of having good people administering the service, (as well as good doctors and nurses), was also highlighted by people who use mental health services. This is not surprising given the level of understanding and sensitivity required from all staff when dealing with people using mental health services.

As with service providers, people using mental health services felt that quality would be enhanced by improved staff morale, staff motivation and good working conditions. People using the services also mentioned that the number of patients/clients staff see in a day affects the quality of the service delivered.

Adults using mental health services said that the value associated with working in the service must be emphasised and that doctors, other professionals involved in the delivery of mental health services and the Department of Health and Children should "*act as champions*". They also raised the issue of staff burnout and felt that staff should not have too heavy a workload since it affects the quality of the service delivered.

Groups representing children and young adults using mental health services emphasised the need to recruit specialists, for example, speech therapists, social workers and counsellors. The groups representing those people using mental health services and who are 'hard to reach' said staff need support. How exactly this support was to be provided was not elaborated upon.

Views of families, parents and carers

Along with the general views on recruitment and retention, families, parents and carers emphasised the issue of burnout, suggesting it causes staff "*to be disrespectful*".

There should be greater flexibility for staff wanting to work across catchment areas, therefore maximising the use of available expertise. In addition to this, the role of the volunteer in the delivery of mental health services should be supported.

Views of organisations with an interest in mental health

Organisations with an interest in mental health stated that the commitment and support of management was key to the delivery of a quality mental health service.

Views of members of the public

When asked about what service providers needed to deliver a quality mental health service, members of the general public said that organisations should provide a physical environment which would "*improve the general well being*" of both staff and people using the service. They also said a rigorous recruitment process should be put in place.

Sub-theme 10.2 — Appropriate staffing levels and expertise

Across all of the stakeholder groups consulted, ***the full complement of a multidisciplinary team was considered critical*** to enable service providers deliver a quality service. (This aspect of quality was also raised by contributors in the context of discussions about the need for a holistic, seamless service, offering the full continuum of care, and reported on in Chapter 3, theme 1). Groups with particular needs, for example, children and people with alcohol and drug problems should be catered for within the multi-disciplinary arrangement. In addition to having the multidisciplinary team in place, it was emphasised that an *inter-disciplinary working* approach was needed. ***(Inter-disciplinary team working was explained as the members of the team working together and sharing expertise, in order to deliver a holistic service).*** There was little difference in the views expressed by the different stakeholder groups. Specific requirements in relation to the multidisciplinary teams, their expertise and how they should work were identified as follows:

Views of service providers

Service providers identified a number of professionals which should be included in the multidisciplinary teams. Those mentioned (order not reflecting importance) included:

- Nurse specialists in mental health/Clinical nurse specialists

- Psychiatric nurses

- Public health nurses

- Counsellors

- Social workers

- Psychologists

- Occupational therapists

- Psychiatrists

- GPs

- Advocates

There was no consistent agreement on exactly who should be on the multi-disciplinary team, but an "*appropriate skills mix and appropriate expertise*" was considered essential. Other general requirements mentioned were people with good interactive skills who "*know how to give quality time to the service user*". Service providers also felt that the multidisciplinary team needs secretarial and administrative support to allow it to work effectively.

The way in which the multidisciplinary team should work was also discussed, for example, using monthly meetings and weekly care conferences to structure and plan the work. Specific areas to be addressed at these meetings were mentioned, including discussions on cases to be referred, case histories and clarification on each professional's role in the treatment plan. Of particular importance was the need for GPs to be involved in these multidisciplinary team meetings. This reflects the strong view of service providers that knowledge and understanding of mental health issues at primary care level needs to be improved.

Views of people using the service

People using mental health services said that an inter-disciplinary approach to working is required. Expertise in dual diagnosis is also required.

Views of families, parents and carers

Families, parents and carers agreed with the need for multidisciplinary teams but added that there needed to be expertise in acquired brain injury and ADHD. They suggested that *a "key worker" be identified from within the multidisciplinary team who would liaise with the families, parents and carers.*

Views of members of the public

Particular areas mentioned by members of the public, where specialist expertise is required, were people with learning disabilities and children. It was also suggested that the multi-disciplinary team should include members with experience in dealing with violence.

As with the other aspects of human resources already described, there was general agreement among the stakeholders consulted regarding the importance of co-ordinated and planned delivery of training and continuous professional development (CPD). The differences lay in the emphasis given to the types of training required and views about why training and CPD were important for the delivery of a quality mental health service.

All the stakeholders felt that ongoing and comprehensive training and CPD was required. All staff should have access to the most up to date methodologies and treatment and also to specialist training for working with people with particular needs. There was a shared view among stakeholders that the incentive should exist for staff to participate in training and CPD. Particular suggestions from the different stakeholders about what should be addressed in training and CPD are detailed below but, overall, training incentives were considered to be extremely important, particularly given the move towards providing a more holistic mental health service.

Views of service providers

Service providers said that *"staff feel empowered through training" resulting in a higher quality service, however they felt that insufficient time was given for training.* Apart from the time needed for training and CPD, funding was also required for staff to attend relevant courses and conferences. Hospital libraries should enable staff to keep up to date with the latest research.

There were several suggestions on ways to approach training. For example, inter-professional and inter-agency training should take place so that knowledge can be shared and an understanding between disciplines can be achieved. Another suggestion was to involve special interest groups in training to provide key insights into the special needs of certain groups of people. Experiential learning and training systems based on staff rotations were also suggested as alternative approaches.

The following were suggested for inclusion in training and CPD:

- Clinical audit

- Supervision training

- Administration

- Team building

- Training on family involvement

- Care planning

- Training to work with people with a learning disability and people with autism

- Assessment techniques

- Ethics, including rights of people using the service, Freedom of Information and informed consent

- Effects of medication

- Training to deliver seamless care (*the specifics of which were not expanded upon*)

- Understanding the dynamics of psychotherapy for professionals referring people to psychotherapists

- A module on deaf user needs, particularly language needs

On a broader level, training for families and people using the service was also mentioned although this aspect of training was not discussed in much detail compared to the training requirement for service providers.

Overall, service providers felt that:

- A good knowledge of mental health issues should exist among service providers and the general public

- A greater awareness of the needs of people using the service should be developed

- Knowledge of discharge planning and the prevention and management of violence was required

- An improvement in attitude towards those with mental health problems should be encouraged

Views of people using the service

Suggestions made by people who use mental health services almost always emphasised **the need for service providers to be trained in the needs of particular groups who use the service.** For example, the need for service providers to be trained to meet the different needs of children with mental illness was emphasised. The need for training in communication skills and inter-personal skills was also highlighted. This is not surprising given the feedback already detailed in Chapter 3 on "Respectful, empathetic relationships". Given that the GP is often the first point of contact for a person using the mental health services, it is not surprising that the GP was highlighted as a professional who required training and CPD in understanding mental health and also being aware of mental health services in the community. For example, it was mentioned by one group that often people are referred by a GP to a psychiatrist too early. This group felt it would be important to improve mental health knowledge and awareness among GPs, and primary care in general, in line with the objective of providing a continuum of care for mental health services.

As with service providers there were specific suggestions for training which are listed below:

- Training for supervisors in occupational centres

- Psychiatric nurse training

- Training for nurse managers

- Training for people working with persons who have particular needs, e.g. people who are deaf, people who are visually impaired, people with physical disabilities, people with dual diagnoses

- Counselling/psychotherapy qualifications for doctors, nurses, psychiatrists

- Spiritual training

- Training for professionals to overcome the stigma associated with mental illness

Voluntary organisations should play a part in training at pre-service level. There should be greater awareness of deaf people in psychiatric hospitals – people who are deaf tend to be hospitalised for longer periods than those who are hearing. There should be six-month training modules in specialised areas concerned with the needs of particular groups. Training and CPD should involve training and talking with other service providers. Similarly, groups representing people who are 'hard to reach' said that training and information is required on different cultures, backgrounds and "life experiences". They also suggested training people from minority, ethnic and homeless backgrounds to work in mental health services.

Views of families, parents and carers

Families, parents and carers felt that **all staff (for example secretaries, cleaners, domestic staff, groundsmen) should undertake training to develop an understanding of mental illness and its impact.** Training should be provided in "person-centred care". Training should also be given to professionals in how to work with people with ADHD and with people who have acquired brain injury. Finally, families, parents and carers suggested there be training in family-based models of recovery and recommended a *"move from a client-centred to a family-centred approach"*.

Views of organisations with an interest in mental health

People involved in the delivery of mental health services understood the impact of poverty on mental health. Training should address the particular needs of children with social and educational needs, or children with disabilities, as well as mental health problems. Staff should also be trained in recognising the signs of child abuse. These organisations also emphasised the need for all staff to engage with and explore the ethos and philosophy of the mental health service. They also suggested that GPs should be trained in alternative treatments for mental health.

Theme 11

Systematic evaluation and review of mental health services, underpinned by best practice, will enable providers to deliver quality services

The sub-themes, relating to this theme, identified during the consultation, include:

11.1   *Evidence based codes of practice*

11.2   *Monitoring and evaluation*

11.3   *Commitment to quality*

Any organisation committed to providing a quality service should ensure that evidence-based best practice drives the development of its services. Almost all stakeholders believe that systematic evaluation and review of services is key to achieving this. The general public were the only stakeholder group who did not raise the issue of best practice or evaluation and review. A common view held was that people using the service should be involved in the review. For example, service providers acknowledged the importance of having effective feedback mechanisms in place.

Sub-theme 11.1   **Evidence based codes of practice**

According to the stakeholders consulted, clear procedures and protocols are required to drive the quality agenda. Specific views from each of the stakeholders are captured below but the message was clear – *all service providers should be striving towards evidence-based codes of practice.*

Views of service providers

Service providers highlighted the need for evidence-based codes of practice, protocols and procedures to underpin a quality service. In particular, they mentioned the need for:

*   Safety protocols

*   Referral protocols, to minimise delays in access and to manage referrals from outside the mental health services

*   Discharge protocols for each part of the service

*   Pharmacy codes of practice

*   Uniform policies across service areas, such as day hospitals

*   Protocols for informed consent

*   Protocols for prioritising people in greatest need

- Communication procedures

- Protocols for response to in-patient suicides

- Operational guidelines for professionals and people using the service

- Inter-agency policies, for example:

  - transport of involuntary patients

  - a co-ordinated approach by two agencies working with a person who is homeless

- Protocols to ensure integration, joint working and assignment of responsibility

- Protocols for managing confidentiality

All codes of practice/protocols should be reviewed and refined on a regular basis. Service providers said that research should constantly challenge how services are delivered. **Service providers should always ask, "Is there a better way of delivering our services?". Service providers should support research and should undertake research on population needs.** There should be a broader understanding of mental health, to cover, for example, therapies and alternative treatments.

A particular issue raised by service providers was confidentiality, for example the level of information which should be recorded in patients' files, i.e. what level of information should be shared among professionals? There needs to be an agreed approach on whether summaries or detailed notes are recorded in the patient file.

Lastly, service providers felt that accountability systems should be in place in all organisations providing mental health services. There should be clinical supervision for all grades, and opportunities for external supervision independent of line management.

Views of people using the service

Standards in services for children should be assessed and they should not be "overly psychiatry-based". This reflects views previously discussed about children and other people using the service needing a more holistic service.

The importance of professionalism when dealing with children was also stressed. "*Service users should know what to expect*" was one comment made highlighting the need for clear communication. National and regional ethics committees, safety codes for families and professionals and protocols are needed for situations where persons are missing from an institution or hospital.

Groups representing people who are 'hard to reach' said that existing values should always be challenged to highlight the needs of the people using the service.

Codes of practice for research (including where it is done, how it is regulated, informing people that they are the subject for research, etc.) should be developed – patients should be informed if they are part of a research project.

Views of families, parents and carers

Families, parents and carers agreed broadly with the other stakeholders regarding standards saying that **there needs to be national standards for mental health services and that these standards need to be enforced through inspection.** They suggested looking at models in the UK. They said that there needs to be codes of practice in relation to restraint – presently, each hospital has their own codes of practice and they felt it would be of benefit for all hospitals to adopt the same codes of practice.

Families, parents and carers identified that codes of practice are needed for:

* Instances where an adult family member refuses to co-operate, take medication etc.

* Dealing with "bad news" in relation to a patient

* Sharing information regarding medication

Families, parents and carers raised the issue of the right of the spouse to confidentiality, for example a spouse refusing consent for the partner to have information about his/her illness.

Research into progressive methods of teaching should be carried out and "thinking outside the box" should be encouraged.

Finally, families, parents and carers felt that codes of practice should be monitored by the Mental Health Commission.

Views of organisations with an interest in mental health

Organisations with an interest in mental health said that information is needed about evidence-based approaches to the delivery of mental health services. They agreed with the other stakeholders about the need for procedures and protocols and felt they needed to be standardised to incorporate best practice.

There were strong views regarding procedures when dealing with children. They felt that hospital ethics committees should pay particular attention to issues surrounding treatment of children and young people. There should be consultation with staff, parents and children to ensure treatment is consistent with the best interests of the child. The legal and moral rights of parents and children to consent to treatment should be defined, understood and respected by service providers. There should also be codes of practice regarding interaction with parents when a child or young person dies. Clear information should be available for children regarding any invasive procedures and other difficult situations. It was felt that discharge policies and procedures for children are particularly deficient at present. Finally, they recommended that "*Every child should be protected from unnecessary mental health care treatment and investigation and should have the right to refuse to participate in medical research*".

Views of members of the public

A specific recommendation from members of the public was to use a centralised file detailing what medication had already been used by each patient to prevent overmedication. This would also facilitate a tracking mechanism for the patient's treatment.

In order to improve the quality of mental health services it was widely agreed that services needed to be monitored and evaluated to establish what is working and what needs to be done differently.

Views of service providers

Service providers suggested using satisfaction checks, both qualitative and quantitative, in the evaluation process.

"Independence is key to effective monitoring and evaluation" and a way in which this can be achieved is through cross health board audits. For example, the director of nursing from one health board could audit the services in another area. Comparisons with other services across catchment areas and with services in other countries was also suggested as a means of learning how to do things better. Evaluation of resource usage (both human resources and funding) should be included in the evaluation.

This stakeholder group felt there should be ongoing independent audit of:

- Facilities, record keeping and information dissemination

- Data such as waiting lists, length of stay in hospital, discharge patterns

- Factors influencing outcomes

- How treatment could be more effective

- Sources of help in difficult cases

- Clinical treatment in line with international standards

The development of performance indicators was also suggested as a way to measure both internal and external customer satisfaction. Outcome measures such as morbidity, mortality and absenteeism rates should be recorded also. Discussion groups, focus groups, interviews and surveys were suggested as feedback techniques and the general view was that users should be involved in the process. There should be a feedback system for all stages of the care process and, most importantly, service providers should act on feedback. In particular, feedback on satisfaction with GPs was mentioned, presumably given the fact that they are often the first point of contact.

Views of people using the service

The views of people using the service were in line with those providing the service. However, people who use the service were keen to point out **the need for a user-friendly complaints procedure.** For example, people using mental health services should be able to speak up about difficulties a person may be having. There should be a feedback, or complaints mechanism which would identify what was, and what was not, working and service providers should "*be willing to learn from mistakes*". Those representing children said that "*outcomes from the service should be measured*". The level of integration of the services should also be included in the review process.

Those involved with people using mental health services who may be 'hard to reach' or marginalised felt that service providers need to acknowledge that the system may not be working. They also expressed strong views about putting in place a sensitive and user-friendly complaints procedure. They pointed out that there had been a big improvement in the complaints procedure for refugees.

People using mental health services said that there was a need for independent auditing and that the Mental Health Commission should monitor the quality of services, both public and private, around the country.

The main message from people using mental health services was that they should be involved in the evaluation of the service.

Views of families, parents and carers

"Ask the patients their views" was the key message from families, parents and carers.

They felt that the ethos from the top must change to a user-centred approach. They also said that more accountability was expected from private providers.

Views of organisations with an interest in mental health

These organisations highlighted the need for effective data for planning and monitoring the services.

Views of members of the public

The feedback from members of the public was that there was no evidence that expectations were being monitored or evaluated. There should be an ongoing assessment of quality with thorough and regular reviews of quality assurance mechanisms. This should include inter-departmental checks.

Feedback mechanisms mentioned were:

- A system for complaining to an independent body

- Conduct surveys

- Ask support groups, volunteer groups and professional groups for their views

- Carry out telephone interviews

- Interview staff of service providers

- Ask the families of those using the service

- Use independent people to obtain the feedback

There should be an acceptance by service providers of the benefits of random and unannounced external monitoring. Service providers should also listen to individual feedback during the course of treatment, for example a person suggesting that the medication be reduced should be taken into account.

Lastly, members of the public mentioned that staff performance and morale should be under constant review.

Sub-theme 11.3 **Commitment to quality**

Not surprisingly, a "*commitment to quality*" was deemed necessary for service providers to improve mental health services

Views of service providers

Service providers suggested approaches to improving quality, such as:

- Accreditation

- Benchmarking

- Risk management

- Independent audit "*by an inspectorate with teeth*"

They also said that clinical supervision (including peer and management supervision) would also help to raise the standards of the services delivered.

Views of people using the service

People using services said that "*quality (mental health services) needs to be defined and then measured*". The values of the service provider organisations may not be the same as those of the people using the services and therefore, it is important to take into account the views of those using the services when developing plans.

Views of families, parents and carers

In addition to the general views expressed already, families, parents and carers suggested that an inspection report should be used to develop an action plan and then followed up. They also felt that there should be minimum standards for residential services. All in all, they felt that there needed to be a cultural change and a *"commitment to providing a world-class service"*.

Views of organisations with an interest in mental health

Organisations with an interest in mental health said that there needed to be a clear focus and direction for service providers and that there needed to be a clear commitment to quality (minimum standards and benchmarking were specifically mentioned) with *"all services regularly and independently audited"*.

Theme 12

The right management systems and structures should be put in place to facilitate the development of a quality mental health service

The sub-themes, relating to this theme, identified during the consultation, include:

12.1 *Management structures*

12.2 *Managing resources*

12.3 *Management processes*

Quality in mental health services will be driven far more effectively if the right structures and systems are in place. Quality must drive the development of effective management processes. At the same time management structures with clearly defined roles and responsibilities, which reflect the quality agenda, will enable staff to understand on a day to day basis how their job plays a part in improving the quality of the services.

During the consultation process almost all stakeholder groups apart from the general public, identified having effective management structures and processes as important for the delivery of a quality service. Service providers in particular felt that there needed to be leadership within the organisations to drive the quality agenda. In addition to this, given the lack of resources available currently for mental health services, stakeholders felt effective management of financial resources was key to helping improve the quality of the service. A number of important points were made by different stakeholders which are captured below.

Sub-theme 12.1 **Management structures**

Across all the stakeholder groups there was a strong view that *service providers require effective structures from the higher levels of management through to the way people are "organised on the ground".*

Views of service providers

Service providers felt there needed to be good leadership to drive quality and lobby for change. There needs to be a clear direction with stated vision, missions and goals, laying out how the organisation is going to improve the quality of the service.

The new structures put in place should "*replace the current triumvirate of medicine, nursing and administration*" and include new disciplines to reflect the multi-disciplinary approach. A sector clinical team manager should be appointed from among the professionals represented on the multidisciplinary team. The new structures should ensure accountability going forward with defined roles, responsibilities and decision making ability. They should also address professional governance issues.

Service providers suggested that the same structures should be set up across catchment areas and health boards, with devolved and local management encouraged. It is important that organisations are not top heavy, for example "*no new departments should be developed as a result of the quality framework initiative*".

All staff should be involved in initiatives and have a say in service planning in organisations. Lastly, service providers felt there should be regional ethics committees put in place.

Views of people using the services

The main issue raised by people using the services, in relation to management structures, was the need for clear areas of responsibility for those delivering the service so that everyone involved knows where responsibilities begin and end.

Views of families, parents and carers

When discussing the need for someone to drive the quality agenda, families, parents and carers pointed out that there would need to be an administrative structure to enable this to happen.

Sub-theme 12.2 **Managing resources**

Protecting budgets was the main concern for those that raised the issue of managing resources. **People felt that, as well as there being inadequate funding for mental health services, the funding available was not being directed to those that needed it the most.**

Views of service providers

Ringfencing of budgets for service provision and also for staffing was considered key to improving the service (this was also mentioned by the general public). Ringfencing budgets for each profession would ensure that non-medical posts on multidisciplinary teams would be protected and vacancies filled, for example "*ringfenced funding was needed for social work posts*".

A strongly held view was the need for resources to be allocated to "*allow people to do their job*" and resources should "*match the needs of the population served*".

There should also be devolved budgets for training. A pilot study for unit budgeting should be set up. Information Technology (IT) systems (for example FACE software) should be funded.

Lastly, value for money should be reflected in how funding is used.

Views of people using the services

The overarching view from people using the services was that resources should be provided to allow services to be provided to the highest standards. Doctors and nurses should be involved in planning and allocating funds and staff in general should drive the value for money agenda.

There was a view expressed that psychiatrists sometimes keep people in hospitals rather than in lower support accommodation, which uses up a lot of the budget unnecessarily.

Sub-theme 12.3   Management processes

There were many suggestions on the management processes that are needed in a quality service. Having effective communication processes in place was raised by a number of stakeholders, including service providers and people using the services. *Access to good information, twenty-four hours a day, seven days a week, enabled by appropriate IT systems, was considered necessary to develop good processes.*

Views of service providers

Service providers felt that a person-centred approach was needed, supported by a person-centred mission and philosophy. The person-centred approach equated to "*less time spent on meetings and less bureaucracy*", although regular meetings for staff with management was also suggested so that staff could influence at management level. It was also stated that front line staff need a knowledge of policies.

Staff should be involved in "innovative" service planning and planning should be linked to national strategies. Planning should enable a degree of certainty about future service development.

People representing the ambulance service felt they should be involved in discussions on how the service should be improved, given their experience and exposure to people with mental illness.

Lastly, a director of information on services was identified as a way of improving management processes

Views of people using the services

As with service providers, people using mental health services said that there is a *need for mechanisms to facilitate communication across all providers to improve quality. A national register of all service providers would be of benefit, for example.*

It was suggested that monitoring of ethnic requirements would help to plan services appropriate to the needs of people from ethnic minorities.

"We need a well organised smoothly running service" sums up the views of those people using mental health services.

Views of families, parents and carers

The views of families, parents and carers were similar to other stakeholders. Particular views expressed were that adequate IT support and equipment was required and that statistics are required about the needs for the future so that effective planning can take place. Management processes should be supported by a vision, mission and goals which "*are made real in the day to day work, as opposed to just stuck up on the wall*". Lastly, families, parents and carers felt that all staff should be consulted about planning services.

There was a view that it is not appropriate that health boards should be providers of services, and funders of services, as this may lead to conflicts of interest.

Views of organisations with an interest in mental health

Specific suggestions related mainly to the planning process for services for children. Data should be collected to assist in the planning and monitoring of services for children. However, special searches are needed to identify all children using mental health services, not only those being treated by child psychiatrists, but also those using therapeutic services, for example.

There should be public access to the annual reports of mental health institutions. There should be clarity of purpose in relation to what services aim to achieve. For example, the "*managing the problem*" approach will achieve less successful outcomes than a "*wellness approach*".

Views of members of the public

As with the other stakeholders, members of the public felt that effective service planning relies on effective data gathering which will result in better managed services.

Theme 13

The external environment, in which the mental health services operate, has an important role to play in developing a quality mental health service

The sub-themes, relating to this theme, identified during the consultation, include:

13.1 *Funding*

13.2 *Public education on mental heath issues*

13.3 *Legislation*

13.4 *Getting mental health on the political agenda*

During the consultation a number of system issues were raised which included things that individual service providers are not in a position to influence fully. Examples include funding, raising public awareness, legislation and the political agenda.

Sub-theme 13.1 **Funding**

The view among all stakeholders was that funding for mental health services should increase.

Views of service providers

A number of suggestions were made by service providers relating to funding. For example, the government should release funds which are *"tied up in institutions"*. Service providers said that funding is required to maintain facilities and provide the full complement of multidisciplinary teams. An example of extra funding needed was for home help – public health nurses currently have a fund for home help; however, psychiatric nurses do not have funding allocated to home help.

Service providers felt that **funding for mental health should be ringfenced** and that there should be less spending on psychiatrists and consultants and more on the actions from the primary care strategy and other national strategies. Another area requiring increased funding was community mental health nursing.

Finally, **the health system needs to address the two tier (public/private) system, where many public patients do not have access to the full range of treatments available.**

Views of people using the services

Similar views were expressed by people using mental health services in terms of increased funding required and abolishing the two tier system. Another issue raised was the over dependency on voluntary organisations.

Investing in mental health services would bring benefits such as higher employment, higher tax revenues (as a result of greater employment) and shorter waiting lists.

People with particular needs, such as deaf people, should be targeted by funding.

Views of families, carers and parents

While agreeing with the basic view of increased funding, families, parents and carers felt that a more rational budgeting system based on need should be adopted and a mechanism to assess capacity and need was required.

Families, parents and carers suggested that people, with long-term mental illness should be given a medical card.

Sub-theme 13.2 **Public education on mental health issues**

Reducing the stigma associated with mental illness was considered a big challenge for the health system. This point was expressed numerous times among different groups and in many written consultations. *The public needs to be educated, not only about mental illness, but also about mental health.*

Views of service providers

Service providers recognised that *health professionals needed to be educated as well as the public, to "ensure that people with mental illness are treated with courtesy and respect".*

Raising awareness and educating people could be done through:

• Local and national media, including television and print media

• Promoting mental health at public gatherings, for example erecting stands at pop concerts and national events (e.g. agricultural shows)

• Communications at work places and schools

Service providers feel there is a need for ongoing review of the factors affecting mental health for different groups (Social changes, such as people moving to different parts of the country without family backup, was cited as an example).

Views of people using the services

People who use mental health services agreed with service providers about the need for greater public awareness. They mentioned, in particular, the need for mental health education in schools. If the stigma associated with mental illness was reduced, they suggested that families might be more supportive. They felt that the media portrayal of mental illness in negative terms needed to be addressed. Finally, a new national mental health strategy needs to be developed.

Views of families, parents and carers

A specific point expressed by families, parents and carers was that people with mental illness should not be accommodated in general hospitals.

Good mental health should be promoted, as well as improving the understanding of mental illness.

Views of members of the public

Members of the public expressed strong views regarding the need to reduce the stigma associated with mental health services. They said that mental health services were often not used on account of the associated stigma.

Specific recommendations included:

- Educating teachers and parents on initial signs of mental illness

- Employing counsellors in schools

- Celebrities playing a role in reducing the stigma for young people

- Encouraging the media to run positive success stories of people living, and coping, with mental illness

- Educating employers on mental health issues

- Trade unions and Chambers of Commerce undertaking public education

- Setting up a national help line

Lastly, concerns were raised over the role of drug companies and their relationships with providers of mental health services, particularly consultants. They questioned whether drug companies were offering treatments that were in the best interests of the public.

Sub-theme 13.3 **Legislation**

There were varying degrees of understanding regarding existing mental health legislation, although there was general dissatisfaction with the legislation as it stands. ***Both service providers and people using the service felt that the legislation should be "rights-based" and that the public "need a proper mental health act".*** Service providers felt that health and safety legislation should be applied to mental health services. There was a view that the disability bill needs to be rights-based and the Mental Health Act needs to address the needs of people with a dual diagnosis.

Sub-theme 13.4 **Getting mental health on the political agenda**

Along with the need for increased awareness and education among the public, many stakeholders felt that the political arena needed to be targeted to improve mental health services.

Views of service providers

Service providers felt there was a ***need for a "political champion" to drive the mental health agenda.*** There needs to be clear direction on mental health policy and appropriate representation on relevant policy groups. For example, the point was made that there is no representative from mental health on the Obesity Task Force (this point was also made by people using the mental health service).

Views of people using the services

"A starting point for improving the quality of mental health services is to implement the mental health actions identified in the primary care strategy". A national standards framework needs to be developed. Health boards should set up mental health groups which could liaise with other groups such as sensory, physical disability and intellectual disability.

Views of families, parents and carers

Families, parents and carers felt a complete overhaul of the system is needed and a new mental health strategy should be developed.

Views of members of the public

Members of the public said that there should be linkages between strategic initiatives. Also, gender issues should be addressed within these initiatives, for example men often find it more difficult to admit to their mental health problems.

Lastly, members of the public, and many of those consulted, expressed very strongly that *"something needs to happen as a result of this exercise – we need results!"*

6 Recommendations

This chapter outlines the recommendations from Prospectus on how the Mental Health Commission should move forward with the quality framework for mental health services. The recommendations draw extensively on the feedback obtained from stakeholders during the consultation. They also reflect Prospectus' own experience in developing and implementing quality frameworks and initiatives in different types of organisations.

6.1 Recommendations for the design of a Quality Framework for Mental Health Services

Recommendations – in relation to *designing* a Quality Framework for Mental Health Services

1 Eight themes should form the foundations for the quality framework for mental health services	**2 Determine the broader support role of the Mental Health Commission in fostering quality in mental health services**	**3 Define a clear scope for the quality framework**
4 Define the themes, standards and measures in the quality framework	**5 Outline clear objectives for the quality framework**	**6 The quality framework must allow for organisational flexibility and accommodate other quality frameworks already in place**
7 The quality framework should be applicable across the full range of services required by people using mental health services, carers and families	**8 The quality framework should promote consistency in the service provided across the country and across service providers**	**9 Anticipate some of the implementation challenges during the development phase**

The feedback obtained during the consultation process, and detailed in Chapters 3, 4 and 5 contains clear messages on the views of different stakeholders involved in mental health in terms of what constitutes quality in mental health services.

Although different stakeholders place varying emphasis on certain components of a quality service, there appears to be a consensus on the *core elements of a quality mental health service.*

Based on the feedback obtained during the consultation process, **a quality mental health service is one which** encompasses the following eight themes (order does not reflect priority):

- Facilitates **respectful and empathetic relationships** between people using the service, their families, parents and carers, and those providing it

- **Empowers people** who use mental health services, and their families, parents and carers

- Provides a **holistic, seamless service** and encompasses the **full continuum of care**

- Is **equitable and accessible**

- Is provided in a **high quality environment**, which **respects the dignity** of the individual, his/her carers and family

- Has **effective management and leadership**

- Is delivered **by highly skilled multidisciplinary teams**

- Is based **on best practice** and incorporates **systems for evaluation and review**

| *Recommendation 1* | **Eight themes should form the foundations for the quality framework for mental health services** |

The eight themes identified above, in relation to a quality mental health service, should form the foundations for the quality framework for mental health services, to be developed by the Mental Health Commission.

In developing a quality assessment or an "accreditation" process for mental health services, the Mental Health Commission should:

- Set explicit standards for each theme

- Define measures for each standard

The standards will describe the desired level of performance of mental health services in relation to that theme.

The measures will be specific metrics used to assess actual performance against each standard.

The table below shows some examples of standards drawing on the information obtained during the consultation process.

Examples of standards and measures by theme
(drawing on examples provided during the consultation process)

Theme	Examples of standards	Examples of measures
Facilitates respectful and empathetic relationships between people using the service, their families, parents and carers and those providing it	Individuals using the service feel they are listened to	• Level of service user satisfaction • Level of complaints by people using mental health services in relation to their views being taken on board by those delivering the service
	People using mental health services have sufficient time with the people delivering the service	• Average duration of consultation/appointment and frequency of visits • Level of complaints relating to duration of consultation/appointment
	More positive societal attitude to mental health – reduced stigma for those using the service	• Views of public on mental health issues, identified from attitudinal surveys • Number of community education programmes in place, which promote positive attitudes towards mental health

Provides a holistic, seamless service and encompasses the full continuum of care	Full multi-disciplinary teams in place (in both the community and acute settings)	• Number/mix of staff on team, e.g.
		  - Psychiatrists
		  - Psychologists
		  - Psychiatric nurses
		  - Community mental health nurses
		  - Social workers
		  - Speech and language therapists
		  - Occupational therapists, etc.
		
		• Waiting time for access to different services

	Accurate timely flow of information relating to the service user, between different teams or service providers	• Admission and discharge policies in place, which cover transfer of service user information • Level of complaints by people using mental health services and service providers in relation to delays in transfer of service user records

Recommendation 2 — Determine the broader support role of the Mental Health Commission in fostering quality in mental health services

In addition to developing and rolling out a quality assessment or "accreditation" process for mental health services, the Mental Health Commission needs to consider the other processes or supports it should put in place to facilitate the development of quality mental health services.

For example, should the Mental Health Commission have a role, and, if so, how should it deliver on this role, in terms of:

- Supporting service providers going through the quality assessment/ accreditation process (e.g. through training or consultancy).

- Developing standard complaints procedures throughout the mental health system?

- Conducting consultation with people using mental health services, their carers and families, on an ongoing basis?

- Establishing a process for "mental health proofing" strategies and policies?

- Ensuring mental health issues are addressed in relevant policy initiatives in health, education, housing etc.?

It is important that, when developing the quality framework for mental health services, the Mental Health Commission looks at the full range of supports it should put in place to foster quality in mental health services.

Recommendation 3 — Define a clear scope for the quality framework

The Mental Health Commission needs to carefully consider the scope of the quality framework, i.e. the range of service providers that will be included in the quality framework for mental health services and in the quality assessment or "accreditation" process. In effect, this involves defining *who are the core providers of mental health services*? For example, are GPs "mental health service providers"? Are career guidance counsellors? Are the Prison Services?

For example, the National Disability Authority has suggested in its submission that:

> *"the framework could apply to all organisations that provide services for persons with a mental illness and mental disorder. In doing so, the framework can become a charter or mark that can be used by a wide variety of different services, such as general practitioners, Citizen Information Centres, social welfare offices, etc.".*

The Mental Health Commission will need to decide if the quality framework and the quality assessment or "accreditation" process will cover all statutory, voluntary and private providers of mental health services. It will also need to consider if and how the framework will apply to:

- GPs, who play a very important role in delivering mental health services

- Individual psychiatrists, counsellors, etc. in private practice

- Government agencies, such as local authorities or training bodies who provide services to the general public, including people who use mental health services.

Normally, a phased approach is taken to implementing quality frameworks. This would mean that the quality framework might be implemented in certain service providers initially, and then rolled out to smaller or more specialist providers.

Recommendation 4 **Define the themes, standards and measures in the quality framework**

When developing the quality framework, and, in particular when defining the themes themselves, as well as the standards and measures to be used in a quality assessment or "accreditation" process, the Mental Health Commission should:

- Draw on the experience of other organisations who have developed quality frameworks internationally and in Ireland (including for example, the National Disability Authority, the Irish Health Services Accreditation Board and the Health Information and Quality Authority). Prospectus recommends that before the Mental Health Commission begins working on the detail of the quality framework for mental health services, it should engage with a number of these agencies to learn from their experiences in relation to the development and implementation of quality frameworks. The Commission should tap into their expertise, on an ongoing basis, as it rolls out the quality framework for mental health services.

- Consider the specific suggestions in relation to measures, included in the written submissions received as part of the consultation. Some useful suggestions on specific metrics were included in submissions in response to the question; "If an organisation providing mental health services wanted to make sure it was doing a good job, what questions would it ask?". The written submissions are a rich source of information which should be exploited by the Mental Health Commission well beyond the publication of this report.

Prospectus recommends that once the Mental Health Commission has developed a draft of the quality framework, it should again consult with the range of mental health stakeholders to get their views on the detailed quality framework. This will ensure that the quality framework for mental health services developed is relevant, appropriate to, and has the support of, the different stakeholders. The Commission should also consider sending copies of the draft quality framework, for comment, to all individuals and organisations who made written submissions during this consultation process.

Recommendation 5 Outline clear objectives for the quality framework

A number of the stakeholders consulted emphasised the need for all involved in the quality framework to be clear on its aims – Why is the Mental Health Commission developing and implementing a quality framework? What will the quality framework achieve?

When developing the quality framework, the Mental Health Commission should clearly define the objectives it wants to achieve with the quality framework. For example, one of the objectives may be to ensure that people using mental health services experience a quality and consistent service across the country and across service providers.

Recommendation 6 The quality framework must allow for organisational flexibility and accommodate other quality frameworks already in place

The quality framework for mental health services must be flexible to reflect:

- The diverse needs of people using mental health services, their families and carers

- The different nature and scale of organisations involved in delivering mental health services (for example, GPs, hospitals, psychiatrists, counsellors, voluntary organisations)

A number of organisations providing mental health services have already implemented quality frameworks. The quality assessment or "accreditation" process for mental health services, developed by the Mental Health Commission, should accommodate and work alongside the quality frameworks already up and running in the different service providers.

Recommendation 7 The quality framework should be applicable across the full range of services required by people using mental health services, carers and families

During the consultation, people using mental health services, their carers and families emphasised that the services they need are many and diverse and that they want a service which looks after them as a whole person, rather than merely treating an illness. The services they need range, for example, from mental health services provided by a GP to inpatient treatment. They include support in relation to housing, employment and education. The services are provided by large state run agencies and by smaller voluntary providers.

The quality framework for mental health services must encourage the development of a holistic, seamless service covering the full range of services. It should be applicable in community based services and acute services, in statutory and voluntary organisations, large and small. It should also assess the quality of the service provided to people using mental health services by other state run agencies (such as local authorities and training bodies). In developing a quality assessment or "accreditation" process for mental health services, the Mental Health Commission should identify standards and measures that touch on the range of different services and service providers involved in mental health.

Recommendation 8	**The quality framework should promote consistency in the service provided across the country and across service providers**

Concerns about variations in the level and quality of mental health services available in different geographic locations and individual service providers were voiced during the consultation process. Implementation of a quality framework for mental health services – and, in particular, assessment of the performance of individual service providers against set standards, as part of the quality assessment or "accreditation" process – will highlight variations in the level and quality of service between service providers and geographic areas, and identify improvements which need to be made to address this situation.

In developing the standards and measures for the quality assessment or "accreditation" process, the Mental Health Commission should be mindful of choosing measures which allow for comparisons across different types of service providers.

Recommendation 9	**Anticipate some of the implementation challenges during the development phase**

Many of the service providers who will be involved in implementation of the quality framework, will be impacted to some degree by the health service reform programme currently underway. So, the quality framework will be implemented in a constantly 'shifting' environment. When designing the quality framework for mental health services, the Mental Health Commission should seek to anticipate some of the implementation challenges often associated with quality frameworks.

For example:

- When identifying measures, the quality framework should focus on metrics for which data is already available or can be gathered relatively easily

- It will be important to get the right balance between checking (e.g. through peer reviews and external assessments) and trusting (e.g. self-assessments) in the assessment process. Experience shows that the self-assessment element of quality schemes is the aspect that often has the most powerful impact on altering performance.

6.2 Recommendations for implementing a Quality Framework for Mental Health Services

Recommendations – in relation to *implementing* a Quality Framework for Mental Health Services

10 Use the quality framework as an opportunity to foster more positive attitudes towards mental health	**11** Use the quality framework as a platform for increasing the profile of mental health in terms of national policies and priorities	**12** There should be ongoing consultation with people using mental health services, their families and carers, and service providers
	13 The quality framework or "accreditation" process should become an integral part of the organisations involved in delivering mental health services	
14 Implementation of the quality framework should focus on results - real improvements in mental health services - more than on process	**15** Use the quality framework to drive changes in mental health policies, practice and structure at local, regional and national level	**16** Visible, committed leadership is essential for implementation of the quality framework

Recommendation 10 **Use the quality framework as an opportunity to foster more positive attitudes towards mental health**

The need to foster a more positive attitude towards mental health issues in general emerged strongly from the consultation process. A more positive attitude towards mental health problems will have benefits for those using the service and those providing it. Many people using mental health services, their families and carers are very conscious of the stigma traditionally associated with mental health services and this can impact on their willingness to seek help.

One of the key objectives of the quality framework for mental health services will be to develop a quality mental health service. In promoting the quality framework, the Mental Health Commission should use the opportunity to explain mental illness and mental health, how a quality service can help people with mental illness and the results that can be achieved - particularly to the general public and agencies involved in providing services (e.g. housing, training) to people with mental illness. This should help to create a more positive and understanding attitude to mental health.

Recommendation 11 | **Use the quality framework as a platform for increasing the profile of mental health in terms of national policies and priorities**

One of the messages emerging from this consultation process is that it is neither practical nor desirable to divorce the development and implementation of a quality framework for mental health services from the level of investment in mental health services and the priority accorded to mental health at national level. Many of those involved in the consultation expressed a view that the Mental Health Commission should be a strong voice for mental health services at national level and should seek to influence national strategies and policies in relation to mental health.

The launch of the quality framework for mental health services will provide the Mental Health Commission with a platform for highlighting the need to prioritise the development of mental health services.

The implementation of the quality framework, and in particular, the required improvements to services which will be identified from the performance of service providers in the "accreditation" process on an ongoing basis, will highlight specific areas in need of investment and identify changes required to policies, structures and systems in mental health. The ongoing assessment of service providers in the "accreditation" process should inform the Mental Health Commission, funders of mental health services and policy makers in terms of where change and/or investment is required and to what extent.

Recommendation 12 | **There should be ongoing consultation with people using mental health services, their families and carers, and service providers**

The Mental Health Commission recognises that this consultation was part of an ongoing consultation process with the different stakeholders in mental health. Its objective is to work in partnership with the different stakeholders in developing and implementing this quality framework.

It is, therefore, essential that the different stakeholders' views are taken on board as the Commission develops the detail of the quality framework and when it is implemented (in order to get feedback on how it works in practice and how it should be refined to deal with any implementation challenges).

The large number of submissions received as part of this consultation, and the quality of the participation in the stakeholder workshops and focus groups, indicates the level of commitment and enthusiasm amongst the different stakeholders to bringing about quality mental health services in Ireland. It is obviously important that this enthusiasm is tapped into, and channelled, by the Mental Health Commission, not just in relation to the quality framework but also more generally.

Recommendation 13	The quality framework or "accreditation" process should become an integral part of the organisations involved in delivering mental health services

Service providers involved in the consultation process emphasised the importance of the quality assessment or "accreditation" process becoming an integral part of how they plan, manage and deliver services, and not a separate "programme" or "initiative" that is managed separately and "on the side".

If successfully implemented, the quality framework should create a culture and environment that permeates the entire service provider organisation and fosters a quality mental health service amongst everyone involved in service provision. It should become part of how everybody "does their job".

In designing the process for implementing the quality framework and, in particular the quality assessment or "accreditation" process, the Mental Health Commission should seek, where practical, to integrate the quality framework with existing processes, jobs and roles within service providers.

Recommendation 14	Implementation of the quality framework should focus on results - real improvements in mental health services - more than on process

One of the messages from the consultation process was the need for the quality framework for mental health services to produce results on the ground soon. As stated earlier, there is a commitment and enthusiasm amongst stakeholders to work with the Mental Health Commission to bring about quality mental health services in Ireland.

A quality assessment or "accreditation" process is one mechanism for driving improvements in mental health services. It is important therefore that any quality assessment or "accreditation" process for mental health services – in terms of how it is designed and implemented – focuses on achieving results. In order to demonstrate its value to the different stakeholders, implementation of a quality assessment or "accreditation" process will need to lead to real improvements in services.

When designing the process for implementing the quality framework, the Mental Health Commission should ensure that:

- The focus of the quality framework, and of any quality assessment or "accreditation" process, is on outcomes and results, as much as process

- The processes put in place within individual organisations in relation to the quality framework are appropriate and encourage the right kind of behaviour and culture.

| Recommendation 15 | Use the quality framework to drive changes in mental health policies, practice and structure at local, regional and national level |

There are a number of established practices within mental health which are not regarded as patient or customer focussed by those using the service. Examples mentioned during the consultation process include:

- Catchment areas restrict the services which people using the service can access. People can find themselves in a situation where they cannot use a mental health inpatient or community based service just down the road, because it is in a different catchment area from their home.

- The rotation of Registrars every six months means a disruption for the client or patient in terms of continuity of care

Ideally, the ongoing assessment of service providers, as part of a quality assessment or "accreditation" process, should prompt changes to structures, practices and policies at local, regional and national level, where change is required to ensure the structures, policies and practices are efficient, effective and client focussed.

| Recommendation 16 | Visible, committed leadership is essential for implementation of the quality framework |

Key to the success of a quality framework is the degree to which senior management visibly drive, and display commitment to, implementation of the quality framework.

In order for the quality framework for mental health services to be successful, the Mental Health Commission will need to drive its development and implementation strongly, at national level. It should work closely with the Health Information and Quality Authority (once established) in this regard.

Visible, committed leadership is also required within each service provider implementing the quality framework. This means that senior management need to:

- Convince their organisation of the benefits of participating in the quality framework

- Lead the preparation for assessments conducted as part of the quality framework

- Prioritise implementation of the improvements identified from assessments

A key challenge for the Mental Health Commission will be to obtain the real and ongoing support of senior management in all mental health service providers for the quality framework.

7 Next steps

Having considered the findings from the consultation process and the recommendations from Prospectus, the Mental Health Commission has decided to:

1. **Engage with other national bodies with a remit in relation to quality and standards,** such as the National Disability Authority, the Irish Health Services Accreditation Board and the Health Information and Quality Authority (once established) to learn from their experiences in implementing system-wide quality. **It will also review quality frameworks** for mental health services **implemented in other countries** to identify lessons for Ireland, in terms of both the design and implementation of the quality framework.

2. **Establish a Working Group to design the quality framework.** The working group will include service providers and organisations representing people using mental health services. In designing the quality framework, the Working Group will draw on:

   - Messages from the consultation process outlined in this report

   - Expert advice from other agencies

   - Models for quality frameworks in health and social services implemented in Ireland and internationally

   The key areas the Working Group will address include:

   - Defining the themes, standards and measures which will make up the quality framework for mental health services

   - Defining the broader support role the Mental Health Commission should have in fostering quality in mental health services

   - Determining how the quality framework, and any quality assessment or "accreditation" process, should be rolled out, including:

     - Which service providers will implement the quality framework, and when

     - The processes that should be put in place within each service provider, and at national level, to support implementation of the quality framework

3. **Establish an International Expert Group to quality assure the output from the Working Group** – consisting of, for example, individuals with international experience of quality frameworks in mental health and Irish experts in quality frameworks.

4. **Consult with stakeholders to obtain their views on the quality framework,** designed by the Working Group and **refine the quality framework,** to take on board the feedback obtained from the different stakeholders. This will involve holding a number of consultations with people using mental health services, parents, families, carers and service providers to get their feedback on:

   - The proposed themes, standards and measures in the quality framework

   - The proposed approach to implementation of the quality framework

These steps will be completed within a reasonably short timeframe (for example, 6 – 9 months) to ensure that the Mental Health Commission capitalise on the momentum created by this consultation process.

Appendices

Appendix 1 – Names of organisations who participated in consultation workshops

- Access Ireland/Refugee Integration Project
- An Garda Síochána
- Association of Refugee and Asylum Seekers in Ireland (ARASI)
- Aware
- Barnardos
- Bloomfield Hospital
- Bodywhys
- Central Mental Hospital
- Children in Hospital Ireland
- Comhairle
- Dublin Simon Community
- Eastern Regional Health Authority
- Focus Ireland
- Health Research Board
- Highfield Hospital Group
- Homeless Agency and Dublin City Council
- Irish Association for Alcohol and Addiction Counsellors (IAAAC)
- Irish Deaf Society
- Irish Prisons Services
- Irish Refugee Council
- Institute of Technology Tallaght Student Union
- Mental Health Ireland
- Midland Health Board
- NAMHI
- National Advisory Committee on Drugs
- National Association for Deaf People
- National Children's Office
- National Disability Authority
- National Drugs Strategy Team
- National Educational Psychological Services
- Newcastle Hospital
- Northern Area Health Board
- North Eastern Health Board
- Out and About Association
- People with Disabilities in Ireland
- Probation Services
- Samaritans
- Schizophrenia Ireland
- St. Stephen's Hospital (SHB)
- South Eastern Health Board
- Southern Health Board
- South Tipperary Mental Health
- South Western Area Health Board
- St. Brendan's Hospital
- St. Patrick's Hospital
- The Alzheimer Society of Ireland
- The Institute of Guidance Counsellors
- Union of Students in Ireland
- Western Health Board

Appendix 2 – Names of organisations who sent in written submission

- Airdnua
- Association of Psychoanalysis and Psychotherapy in Ireland
- Blanchardstown Child and Family Centre
- Bodywhys
- Centre for the Care of Survivors of Torture
- Children in Hospital Ireland
- Church of Scientology
- Clontarf Carers Group
- Cluain Mhuire Service
- Community Mental Health Centre, Tullamore, County Offaly
- Consumer Association of Ireland
- Eastern Vocational Enterprises Ltd.
- Irish Association for Counselling and Psychotherapy
- Irish College of General Practitioners
- Irish Society for the Prevention of Cruelty to Children
- Larine Court Resource Centre
- Mental Health Nurse Managers Ireland
- National Council for the Professional Development of Nursing and Midwifery
- National Suicide Review Group
- National Disability Authority
- Northern Area Health Board Centre for Nursing Education
- New Century House
- New Dawn Training Centre
- Newcastle Carers Group
- Rehab Group
- Rialto Community Network
- Roslyn Park College
- Samaritans Irish Regional Office
- Schizophrenia Ireland Lucia Foundation
- Social Workers in Adult Mental Health (Special Interest Group of the Irish Association of Social Workers)
- Association of Speech and Language Therapy (Special Interest Group in Mental Health)
- St Vincent de Paul Society
- Telephone Helpline Association
- The Harvest Centre
- The Mental Health Alliance
- Tulla Hill Hostel
- University College Cork Students Union
- University of Ulster Students Union
- Western Care Association
- Women's Aid

Note: A total of 239 written submissions were received by the Commission as part of this consultation process. The names of individuals who made submissions have not been listed above in order to protect confidentiality.

Appendix 3 – Plans and strategies reviewed

- A Strategic Framework for Mental Health in the Eastern Region (2003-2010)

- Best Health for Adolescents – Get Connected (Developing an adolescent friendly health service) National Conjoint Child Health Committee (2000)

- Focussing Minds – Developing Mental Health Services in Cork and Kerry (Southern Health Board, July 2002)

- Mental Health Commission Strategic Plan 2004-2005

- Mental Health in Primary Care (ICGP, SWAHB, 2004)

- Mental Health in the North East – Towards a Quality Service (5 Year Strategic Plan) (1999)

- National Disability Authority (NDA) – Working together for equality mental health services (July 2004)

- Planning for the Future (Department of Health and Children, 1984)

- Primary Care – A New Direction (Department of Health and Children, 2001)

- Proposed model for the delivery of a mental health service to people with intellectual disability (Irish College of Psychiatrists, July 2004)

- Quality and Fairness – A Health System for You (2001)

- Recovery in Practice (Schizophrenia Ireland, 2003)

- Report of the Working Group on Child and Adolescent Psychiatric Services (Department of Health and Children, June 2003)

- Report of the Working Group on Child and Adolescent Psychiatric Services (Department of Health and Children, February 2001)

- Shaping a Healthier Future (1994)

- Traveller Health – A National Strategy 2002-2005

- Your Views About Health – Report on Consultation for Quality and Fairness – A Health System for You (December 2001)

Appendix 4 – Consultation questionnaire

Public Consultation

The Mental Health Commission is an independent statutory agency set up in 2002. One of its functions is to promote high standards of care within the mental health services.

The Commission has commenced work on developing a system for continuously improving quality in mental health services, which will encourage and foster high standards of care. Mental health services include services for children and adolescents, adults of all ages and persons with an intellectual disability and a mental illness.

The purpose of this public consultation is to gather views as to what high quality in mental health services means, and what factors influence and shape the quality of those services:

- What makes up a high quality service for those who use the services?

- What do families expect from the services?

- What factors have the greatest influence on the work of people delivering the services?

- What aspects of the way in which a service organisation is managed will make the biggest difference to the quality of service?

We are also asking members of the public to tell us about good experiences with mental health services, so that we can build on those good experiences.

Question 1:   *Do you know someone who has had a really good experience of mental health services? What made that experience good?*

Question 2:   *In your view, what makes up a high quality service for those who use the services? (For example, having information about where to get a service, relationships with the person or people giving the service, quality of care, and after-care, etc.)*

Question 3:   *In your view, what do families expect from the services? (For example, knowing where to get advice or help, easy access to a service, being treated with respect, etc.)*

Question 4:   *In your view, what factors have most influence on the quality of the service given by the people delivering mental health services? (For example; training, opportunities for teamwork, codes of practice, etc.)*

Question 5:   *In your view, what aspects of the way in which a service is organised will make the biggest difference to the quality of service?*

Question 6:   *If an organisation providing mental health services wanted to make sure it was doing a good job, what questions would it ask?*

Question 7:   *Have you any other views on what quality in mental health services means?*

Returning the consultation form

Please return the Consultation form to:

Mental Health Commission
St. Martin's House,
Waterloo Road,
FREEPOST
Dublin 4

Latest date for receipt of your views is Friday, July 23rd 2004

In order to help capture the different views of the various interested parties, it would assist us if you would indicate if this submission is from:

A member of the public
A person who is using or has used a mental health service
A carer or family member
A person involved in delivering mental health services
An organisation

If you would like us to send you a copy of the report from this consultation, please give us a name and postal address, alternatively a copy of the report will be available on our website (www.mhcirl.ie).

Name:

Address:

Thank you for taking the time to participate in this consultative process; your input is very much appreciated.

Appendix 5 – Mental Health Commission and Prospectus team members involved in the consultation process

Steering Committee Members

- Annie Ryan, Commission Member

- Bríd Clarke, Chief Executive Officer, Mental Health Commission

- Patricia Gilheaney, Director, Standards and Quality Assurance, Mental Health Commission

- Gerry Cunningham, Director, Tribunals, Mental Health Commission

- Dr. Teresa Carey, Inspector of Mental Health Services, Mental Health Commission

- Ray Mooney, Director, Corporate Services, Mental Health Commission

- Fiona Keogh, Research Consultant, Mental Health Commission

- Rosemary Smyth, Training and Information Officer, Mental Health Commission

- Katie Burke, Director, Prospectus

- Ann Colgan, Associate, Prospectus

- Justine McCarthy, Manager, Prospectus

Prospectus team

- Katie Burke

- Vincent Barton

- Ann Colgan (Associate)

- Justine McCarthy

- Breeta Allen

Mental Health Commission team

- Bríd Clarke

- Gale Gilbert

- Patricia Gilheaney

- Marie Higgins

- Máire McLoughlin

- Des McMorrow

- Ray Mooney

What constitutes a quality service for people using mental health services?

Themes and sub-themes emerging from the consultation

1 The provision of a holistic seamless service and the full continuum of care, provided by a multidisciplinary team	2 Respectful, empathetic relationships are required between people using the services and those providing them	3 An empowering approach to services delivery is beneficial to both people using the services and those providing them
1.1 Continuum of care	2.1 Understanding and empathetic relationships	
1.2 Choice and range of interventions or treatment options at any given stage	2.2 Respectful relationships	
1.3 Community-based services	2.3 Reducing stigma	
1.4 A seamless service		
1.5 A full multidisciplinary team to deliver the service and interventions at every stage		
4 A quality environment, respecting the dignity of the individual and the family, will result in a more positive experience	5 Easy access to services is key to a quality service	6 Receiving a skilful service and high standards of care are extremely important people using mental health services
	5.1 Information	
	5.2 Equitable access and ease of access	
	5.3 Flexible service	

What constitutes a quality service for families, parents and carers?

Themes emerging from the consultation

7 Families parents and carers need to be empowered as team members, receiving information and advice, as appropriate	8 Effective family support services need to be in place to reflect the important role families, parents and carers play in a person's healing	9 Families parents and carers need to experience understanding, empathy and respect